the BIG
WAVE
METHOD

8 Steps to Overcoming Your Fear
and Achieving Your Ultimate Dream

MARK VISSER

HAY HOUSE, INC.
Carlsbad, California • New York City
London • Sydney • Johannesburg
Vancouver • New Delhi

Published and distributed in the United States by: Hay House, Inc.: www.hayhouse.com® • *Published and distributed in Australia by:* Hay House Australia Pty. Ltd.: www.hayhouse.com.au • *Published and distributed in the United Kingdom by:* Hay House UK, Ltd.: www.hayhouse.co.uk • *Published and distributed in the Republic of South Africa by:* Hay House SA (Pty), Ltd.: www.hayhouse.co.za • *Distributed in Canada by:* Raincoast Books: www.raincoast.com • *Published in India by:* Hay House Publishers India: www.hayhouse.co.in

Cover design: Rhett Nacson *Interior design:* Karim J. Garcia

Cataloging-in-Publication Data is on file with the Library of Congress

Hardcover ISBN: 978-1-4019-5320-1

10 9 8 7 6 5 4 3 2
1st edition, October 2017

Printed in the United States of America

To my wife, Jacqueline,
my family, and all my friends who
have been there to support me on this
adventure. I know many of my ideas
came across as crazy at first, but
either way, you guys were always
there and loved me for me no
matter what. Thank you.

CONTENTS

PREFACE

Set your course by the stars, not by the lights of every passing ship.

— OMAR N. BRADLEY

Each of us has a "Big Wave"—a dream that seems to be at the edge of what's possible for us, resonates deeply in our hearts, would require us to concentrate all our energy to accomplish, and—if successful—would transport us beyond who we thought we were. Thing is, often there's a lot of fear standing between us and that dream. There's action that has to be taken between determining a goal and conquering it. And that's where most people get stuck.

The Big Wave Method maps out eight steps to overcoming our fear and making our vision real—steps I developed that helped me conquer my own Big Wave: night-surfing at Jaws in Maui, the most treacherous wave in the world.

Just like me, you likely have an extraordinary dream or goal that you believe is possible—but it's still big enough to feel slightly out of reach. I hope you'll see my story as an inspirational boost for your dream that offers inspiration as well as step-by-step advice, whether you're a fledgling entrepreneur, a first-time marathon runner, an amateur filmmaker, or a would-be author. You know beyond a shadow of a doubt that you have a uniquely creative dream to fulfill—a worthy goal to achieve. That said, this method is equally applicable to the businesspeople I often encounter at my corporate speaking events: C.E.O.s, bankers, lawyers, doctors, and coaches who stand in line to confide in me about their hopes, fears, and big ideas about taking their business to the next level.

The Big Wave Method is the perfect companion for anyone who needs inspiration to take the big risk and do the big thing; anyone who is afraid they'll look back at their life and say, "I could have done something extraordinary. Why didn't I try?"

Don't take your dreams to the graveyard with you. Set them free, and set yourself free in the process.

No matter the dream, no matter the size, there is always a method to achieving what seems impossible.

Are you ready?

CHAPTER 1

JUST A
NORMAL KID

---

*One of the virtues of being very young is that you
don't let the facts get in the way of your imagination.*

— SAM LEVENSON

Ever since I was a kid, I dreamed of being as fast and as tall as Michael Jordan. But when I asked my mum if I was going to be six-six and *be like Mike,* she told me I wouldn't. I remember thinking, *This really sucks.*

I thought if I was not going to be above-average genetically or have other physical attributes of these other people that I worshipped like Muhammad Ali or other professional sports people I'd seen on TV, then I was going to have to settle for an average life. When I looked around, I saw other people excelling at the things they wanted to do. I also assumed they had something I didn't—some secret edge, a gift, or a lot of money that made them appear successful.

I also noticed at a very young age that many success-ful athletes had overcome difficult childhoods or back-grounds, and that gave them a hunger that drove them to be successful. Others seemed to have been brought up with a silver spoon, given every opportunity. Though I wanted to succeed in life and had a great imagination, I couldn't relate to either of those extremes; I didn't have a difficult background, and I didn't come from a wealthy home.

Over and over, I'd think to myself, *What if I'm just a normal person? Could I get far in life just being normal—being myself? Could I do something really special too?* I had never heard a success story of someone who was *normal.* I just knew I wanted to do amazing things, so I'd have to find a way—or make one.

The third of four kids, I wasn't the first, and I wasn't the last. I was there in the middle, superaverage in a way among my family. Maybe it is the middle-kid syndrome, or maybe I just knew I was meant to do more.

And apparently I was a stubborn kid.

My mum says I never really learned to walk. One day, when I was eight months old, I got up and started to run—a little terror. If I saw a family member do some-thing, I'd repeat their actions, teaching myself. You can imagine how great that was when I watched my father make a fire and I went back in the house and repeated what I'd just learned.

Growing up on a farm in country Victoria, Australia, we were surrounded by other farms—hours away from the nearest beach. Once a year, we would go on vacation to a beach. I thought the beach was so cool, but I was afraid of the water, having nearly drowned in a sheep's trough when I was a child.

One afternoon, when I was two years old, I was walk-ing around the farm, watching the sheep and cows, and I dropped my peach in the sheep's trough, which was a

55-gallon drum cut in half. There were several of them along the fence line. The only other form of water we had was a dam that created a pond. You dug a hole into the ground and filled it with water so the cattle and sheep could drink it. That was our version of a swimming pool.

I dived in after my peach, but the water was over my head. So there I was, totally submerged, sitting on the bottom of the sheep's trough. Thankfully, my older brother pulled me out by my hair before I drowned. My mum says I wasn't even fazed; I was still happily eating my peach when I was pulled out. I didn't know to be afraid of the water or that I'd done something wrong, until everyone told me, "That's dangerous. You can't do that." Up until that day, I was fear-free. We are all born fear-free, but as children we are taught to fear, usually for good reason. But then we have to spend the rest of our lives trying to unlearn that fear so that we can live in the moment, as we did when we were children.

One year later, I had another incident involving water that rattled me to the core and caused me to be afraid of the ocean. I was walking with my mum, holding her hand, on the beach while on family vacation. Out of nowhere this shore break grabbed me by the legs and sucked me out. It brought me back to being stuck at the bottom of the sheep's trough and being taught to fear it. In reality, it wasn't that bad of an undertow, but it had enough power to knock me off my feet.

I remember looking up at the beach in front of me. Mum was only three feet away, but it seemed like a mile to me. I was thinking I was going to die, and she was just standing there laughing, like, "You're okay."

I jumped to my feet and ran back to the dry sand, kind of rattled that Mum didn't understand my fears. That thing had nearly killed me!

Now, as a parent of a four-month-old girl, if my kid got dumped by a shore break and I was standing right there, I'd probably be laughing too, especially if she was a cheeky little kid like I was.

But that experience made me believe that the ocean wasn't safe. In fact, I had such a fear of the water, I didn't even learn to swim properly. I took swim lessons when I was nine, but several lessons in, the instructor told my mum, "Your son can't keep up. He can't be in the class." I was so scared of the water—especially the deep end of the pool—that I couldn't concentrate on the lessons and I panicked while practicing my strokes.

Aside from being sucked out by the ocean and nearly drowning (in my mind, anyway!), I have great memories of being on vacation at the beach. All I ever did was build sand castles and play in the shoreline in ankle-deep water. Maybe once or twice I'd go out to my knees and get a whitewash, a completely broken wave, and it would come through while I'd lie on my boogie board or surf mat, and I'd let it push me into the shore. And because I was never fully submerged, over time I forgot about my fear of drowning.

Beach time was a really fun time for our family. When you got a hot dog for lunch and visited the beach every day, it was pure bliss. My family moved to the beach in Queensland just before my 10th birthday. I joined what's called Nippers, which is a junior lifesaving class. There were several events for the kids, one of which was called Flags, where the kids sprint across the sand to pick up a flag, which was really a 12-inch piece of garden hose wedged in the sand. There was also a swimming event and a paddling event.

Although I wasn't comfortable in the water, I was fast on my feet, and I won the Flags race. That helped dull the sting a bit for the swim portion of the event, when I came in dead last. The next event was a board paddle, and I had to get pulled out halfway through it. I had no upper-body strength and was so timid. I got absolutely annihilated by every other kid. But I'd won the foot races, so that was enough to give me hope that I could improve.

My parents didn't have guaranteed work situations in place, but they wanted us to experience a better life. We soon settled into our new location and thrived in the environment. They were very supportive of us kids doing what we loved doing, and I loved the *idea* of surfing, but no one in our family surfed. I would watch the surfers—some were kids my age (or a bit younger), others were teenagers, and some were adults, but they all looked pretty strong to me. Their mums weren't even with them! I'd watch them paddle out and think, *Wow! They're going out way past waist-deep. How cool is that?* They were riding waves that seemed so big, and because of my fears, I had to be content riding my little bodyboard in knee- or waist-deep water. I'd watch them and be mesmerized.

Despite my fear, I had a desire in me. *I was drawn to the ocean.* My guess is that you've felt this sensation before too—being both terrified of something and intrigued by it at the same time.

Every time I was near the water, I felt a great force pulling me toward it, as though the ocean were someone I had known for a long time. I would sit at the shore, and I would feel at peace in a way I didn't feel anywhere else. But then, of course, my mind would take over once I hit the water's edge.

When we moved to the beach, instead of thinking about my fear all the time, I was able to focus on the fun we'd had there on holidays. My feelings about water began to change. Plus, because I didn't go in over my head, I was always in control, it felt easy, and the water was warm.

CATCHING MY FIRST WAVE

Soon after we'd moved to the Queensland area, I was playing on the shore one day when a guy's surfboard washed in. I grabbed it and tried to bring it to him. Instead he said, "Oh, you can have a wave."

I'd been watching the surfers for several years by then, so I knew what to do. I walked out to waist-deep water—not too deep—where the fully broken white-washes would roll through. The whitewash is even smaller than a small wave going into shore—the easiest part of the wave, and the part all surf instructors put beginners on as they learn to surf. I positioned myself in front of the whitewash and caught it, and I actually stood up on the board on my very first attempt. I rode it in until the fins hit the sand, and I was still standing on the board, thinking I was killin' it. The whole thing was probably a four-second ride, but from then on, I was hooked. I was so proud of myself for standing up on a wave on my first try.

From the shore, only minutes earlier, it had seemed like an unachievable thing. I'd looked out into the ocean and had seen all these people riding waves, filling me with such happiness. Then I'd think about how I sucked at swimming and how I was scared of the water, and decide that surfing wasn't going to be possible.

But that day, standing on the beach with the biggest grin on my face after riding my first wave, I thought, *Holy shit, I just did that!*

When my 11th birthday came along, I told my parents I wanted a surfboard. My mum thought I was biting off more than I could chew, and in a way she was right, but that's what looking at the ultimate stretch is. It's when you are saying you want something that you are not certain you can actually have.

My mum suggested a newer-model bodyboard instead, but I stood firm. I knew what I wanted. I remembered the experience of how cool that first wave was, and I also knew it would stretch my limits. I still feared the water, but I knew that if I got a board, I would be forced to go out past the shoreline.

My first surfboard was a piece of crap—it had been snapped in half and repaired with a big dirty resin line across the middle where the fiberglass had been fixed. But it had three fins instead of one, and that was all I cared about! Even so, I was still doing what I'd done before on my bodyboard—only now I was surfing in waist-deep water. I still wasn't like those other kids, the ones who were paddling way out. As I became more familiar with surfing, however, I slowly developed the confidence to try to go one step farther—and then another.

At that time, the coolest thing in my mind was to be able to catch an unbroken wave. I had ventured out past the shoreline, but I still wouldn't go out over my head. One day I paddled out, and there was nothing on the shore for a while. So I had to paddle a little farther, though I was nowhere near out the back, which is where the farthest-breaking waves are. I caught a whitewash again. When I stood up, the whitewash reformed into an unbroken wave. I thought, *Holy crap! I'm on an unbroken wave!* It had probably only been for a second, when the whitewash went higher and showed a bit of open face on the wave, but to me it felt like I'd finally ridden an unbroken wave. I went straight in and thought I was a hero. I was so stoked, thinking I'd done the impossible!

Someone mentioned that I'd need a smaller board if I ever wanted to get better and progress beyond riding small whitewashes. I got another secondhand surfboard for Christmas. This one had been snapped across the nose and had a brown repair line, but the rest of the board had cool colors on it—black-and-orange pinstripe rails. It was also more modern and cooler than my first board.

On small days, when the waves, top to bottom, were maybe two feet tall, I started taking chances and paddling out past the shore. But it took a whole year of surfing whitewash to get me past that point. I became a little bit stronger, but I still always stayed where I could touch the bottom.

Then one day it happened. I was planning on staying closer to the shore. There were no waves, so I kept paddling out until I was about 50 meters offshore, where the rest of the surfers were. Then suddenly the unbroken waves came and I was superscared. *What do I do?* I thought. I started paddling back in and let one wave break in front of me. But then I turned around and got smashed by another, and it washed me in a bit. I panicked and untangled my leg rope as I pulled myself onto the board and kept paddling in. The next whitewash came, but it wasn't that intense. This was what I had feared, and now that it had happened, I realized it wasn't as bad as I had imagined.

My friends at school who surfed were the ones who really helped me get over my fear of deeper water. Their older brothers had taught them everything, and surfing was normal to them. When I'd paddle out with them, I felt safer.

My friends would take off on five-foot waves, and I thought they were crazy! I didn't want any part of that—I wanted a nice, easy wave. But little by little I chipped away at my fear by trying bigger waves.

DREAMING THROUGH DOUBTS

Now that I was practicing often, I began competing in surfing contests. I was 13, in my first year of high school, and I had more testosterone, along with a more macho attitude of being willing to give new things a go. I had yet another new secondhand board, and this time it didn't have any repair marks or creases on it. It looked like it was only a few years old, which was a big deal to me. And it was definitely faster.

A school surfing contest came up. I had no idea what it would be like, but it was part of the school curriculum to get involved and active. The very first competition I entered, I came in dead last. I had no idea what I was doing, and it was overwhelming.

I was really good at AFL football, which is Aussie Rules. That was my main sport during weekends and what I trained for during the week. I had been the captain of the junior team several years in a row, and I'd won "best and fairest" at the state carnival when we were up against all the other best teams in the state. We'd even won our last grand final with a score of 102–3. There was no competition in Queensland at the time, and I presumed I'd have a great career in the AFL (Australian Football League). But even though I was really good, and it took up most of my time and energy, I wasn't very excited about it. Surfing was a different kind of challenge.

Coming in dead last at competitions stung, but it didn't dampen my enthusiasm for surfing. Instead it made me determined to get better and practice more.

I practiced more and tried new moves. The next competition I entered—a full year later—I got fourth in the finals! I began to enter more competitions and got to several final rounds. A local surf shop even sponsored me, and they gave me a free T-shirt, some stickers to put on my board, and five free blocks of wax, which were worth about $2 each. But I was sponsored!

I entered a competition called "Searching for the Stars" at Kirra Beach on the Gold Coast. The highest-placed unsponsored surfer (meaning those without a major clothing sponsor . . . my wax blocks didn't count since they were worth about $10) got a significant sponsor. If you had a proper sponsor, you would be dressed from head to toe in their gear and have their logo on the nose of your surfboard. A proper sponsor would also make a financial commitment to you and pay for your flights and entry fees into contests, as well as supply you with their products. I placed fifth in that competition, but I was the highest-placing unsponsored surfer, which gave me even more incentive to improve.

By the time I was 15, I had a few sponsors and was fully addicted to surfing. I'd ride down to the beach with my surfboard on my bike rack, going before school every morning and after school every afternoon. On weekends, I woke up at 4 A.M. to ride down to the beach. I wanted to better myself all the time. I wanted to turn my dreams into reality.

Though I was the most determined, I was never "the best." I made representative teams, but if there were six guys getting picked, I was number five. Even if I won an event, I felt like there was always a question mark beside my name. Sometimes I had flashes of brilliance, when I would go out and surf and think I was really good. Then I might be thrown into an environment with a lot of surfers and have an absolute shocker where I couldn't get it together. So, even though I believed I was really good, I couldn't prove it.

I was still frustrated by the thought of being normal, held back by my limiting beliefs that I wasn't good enough to succeed or hadn't earned the right to succeed somehow. I didn't necessarily want to prove what I could do to other people, but I wanted to prove to *myself* that I was capable of doing something well.

I wanted to own my own space in life.

As scary as it is, there's great value in tackling your Big Wave. Some of these benefits are obvious, such as embracing the feeling of success, taking charge of your own life and destiny, expanding your boundaries, and enhancing your life. Other benefits are more subtle, but equally important, like self-validation, self-worth, growing your confidence, and being an example to those who've watched your journey.

WHAT IS A "BIG WAVE"?

In surfing, a big wave is one that is at least 20 feet high, and a big-wave event doesn't run unless the waves are a minimum of about 30 feet face height. It's massive, daunting, and being able to ride one successfully is a goal for many. I'll never forget my very first Big Wave experience.

I was on Oahu at Waimea Beach in Hawaii in December 2004. The most prestigious big-wave event of its time, the "Eddie Aikau," had just finished. After watching it all day, I paddled out after the event had just finished and got a wide "set wave." Everyone else was out of position for that one but me.

For a young, non-local guy to get a good wave like that without getting dropped in on was pretty much a miracle! Sometimes locals can get annoyed at people visiting Hawaii. From a Hawaiian's point of view, you're in their waters to get their waves, and they have the right-of-way—and rightfully so. So if they see a non-local trying to catch a good wave, they're likely to drop in on you, even if you're a well-known surfer. I've seen Kelly Slater get burned all the time on waves like that. But it's also just crowded—there are so many surfers, it's common to see three or four guys on every wave. That's particularly true at Waimea.

The wave I rode was about 15 to 18 feet high, with a 25- to 30-foot face. At the time it was the biggest wave of my life by a long shot, and that was the moment that set the Big Wave fire alive in my heart.

Now, you don't have to be a surfer to have a Big Wave! Your Big Wave might be starting a business, running your first half-marathon, adopting a child, or moving across the country to a city you've been in love with for years. These are worthy dreams. They may take massive effort to achieve, scare the shit out of you, drain your bank account, or require maximum physical effort—but they're totally worth it.

I believe each person is born with a Big Wave dream inside them. It's up to us to recognize it, prepare for it, and go after it with our whole hearts. Life's too short to play it small.

Your dream will stretch you. You'll have to become the best human you can be in order to achieve it. At times, you'll have to believe in the impossible, when you can't see the end of the path from where you're currently stand-ing, and you can't seem to find the answers to the problem you're trying to solve. At times like this, you have to stand anyway. Believe in yourself anyway. Believe in your goal anyway. It sets you free to believe that nothing is impos-sible for you.

WHAT ARE THE DANGERS
OF AVOIDING YOUR BIG WAVE?

If you're anything like me, you dread the feeling of being average forever. I just knew that I had it in me to do more with my life than the options that surrounded me every day. But along with that desire for more, I also battled with limiting beliefs.

I wanted to do great things, but I'd doubt myself. *Why should I be any different from everyone else? Why do I deserve more?* That thinking alone kills more dreams than you can imagine. Negative thinking leads you to ignore that stirring in your heart, the pulsing light inside trying to get out.

The result is that you walk through your 20s, 30s, and 40s becoming more and more numb to your dream. Making up excuses and finding reasons as to why you can't make that career change. Why you shouldn't spend an extra hour each day training for that event. And why you wouldn't be successful anyway, even if you tried.

You might think you're being mature, responsible even, in "giving up" on the dream. But that's not true at all. Fear is guiding your thoughts. That one four-letter word is the only thing that can keep you living the exact same life 10 years from now. It's the only thing that can stand in the way of living the life you've always dreamed of living.

You have two options: One day, you'll look back with regret and wonder, "What if?" and it will haunt you for the rest of your life. Or you'll look back in gratitude and think, *Thank God I made that decision!* because you know you are truly living your dream, thanks to some hard work and a willingness to take a risk.

Yes, fear is a very real dream-killer. I've struggled with it throughout my whole life. The thing is, fear can actually be your friend. You can use fear to make you extremely aware of your surroundings and circumstances. With practice you can reverse the negative or paralyzing effects of fear with intentional thinking, positive affirmation, and action, and let fear do its real job of protecting you and making you better.

HOW DO YOU KNOW
IF IT'S YOUR BIG WAVE?

So you're pumped up and ready to take control of your life, right? How do you know if this dream of yours—your Big Wave—is really worth tackling?

Here are some questions to help you gauge whether this is a passing thought or a deep-down desire.

1. Does this dream resonate with your heart?

2. Does it generate a certain amount of fear?

3. Would it take you outside of your everyday reality?

4. Although some people would say it's impossible, do you, on some level, believe it's achievable?

5. Will it take planning and strategizing and preparation?

6. Will it inspire you to become the best you can be?

7. Will it bring you joy?

8. If you never try to achieve this goal, will you regret it?

If it's your Big Wave, you would have answered yes to most, if not all, of these questions. The truth is, if you can walk away from a dream, having never tried to accomplish it, and without any regrets, it was never really your dream in the first place.

But when you have a true dream, the internal message is the same, regardless of what your Big Wave is. You want to do it. You *need* to do it. You have to do it!

You might be . . .

- A lawyer taking on a seemingly impossible legal case

- A real-estate agent wanting to increase sales by 20 percent in a down market

- A busy parent determined to sit down and actually write a book

- An amateur filmmaker who wants to create a feature-length film

- Someone wanting to lose weight and get healthy

- A newbie athlete deciding to run a marathon or do a triathlon

Every single one of these dreams is valid and worth achieving. You know it can be done because you've seen or heard of other people who have done it. The only thing that separates you from the people who've already accomplished their dream is that they've taken action. The great thing is, there's probably a tried-and-true road map already out there for your exact dream! You don't even have to create one from scratch or reinvent the wheel. You just have to find a method that is proven to work, make the necessary changes for your specific circumstances, and get going.

It sounds a bit cliché, but I think it's important for each person to follow his or her heart and do specifically what is right for him or her. What's right for me and what's right for you could be two different things. Only you know what feels good, and what is right for your soul. You know when you are working in the flow of what you stand for as a person.

When I decided I wanted to be a professional surfer, people said that was unlikely, but I didn't listen. When I decided I wanted to try to surf Jaws at night, people said it couldn't be done, but I did it anyway. Each time doubts came up, I applied a simple strategy that works for any big dream. I've used it time and time again with each new obstacle I have been faced with.

You can use these exact same principles to tackle your dream, bit by bit:

1. Break the process down into bite-size pieces.

2. Brainstorm ways around each obstacle.

3. Follow through with your plan and overcome all those obstacles, one step at a time.

4. Examine and overcome your fears.

This may seem like an oversimplified guide to achieving your goals, but as you'll see, we often tend to make things harder than they really are.

CHAPTER 2

FOLLOWING WHAT
FEELS GOOD

---

*The most powerful weapon
on earth is the human soul on fire.*

— FERDINAND FOCH

You might have already discovered a part of your passion. If so, that's awesome. But be aware that you have to go through many layers to get to your ultimate goal. Each one is important because it will teach you something about the process and about yourself.

In my teenage years, I'd started off as a small-wave surfer, participating in local events and doing fairly well. I improved each year and gained bigger and better sponsors. But at some point, I began to lose the passion for small waves. At first I was confused. Why didn't I love this anymore? I loved surfing, but I didn't enjoy catching a knee-high wave that went straight into the sand and had no power. It wasn't fun anymore.

We'd fly all over the world and we'd be out there for a 20-minute heat to do as many wiggles as you could before your fins hit the sand, and that was what determined your career. I had been going at it hard for three years when surfing no longer felt exciting. I was seeing some success, but not enough to really give me a sense of fulfillment.

Eventually I realized that I hadn't lost my passion for surfing at all. I had merely realigned and redirected my dream. I discovered that what I really wanted was to surf big waves—and a broken toe helped solidify that passion.

By 2005 I had spent a whole year going against the grain trying to make it in the small-wave World Qualifying Series (WQS) Tour. I'd start off in the first round because I didn't have a seeding. When you start in the round of 300 and something, making three or four rounds feels like progress, but it's still a mile from the top. A few times I'd get through to the round of 64, which was a good result, but it wasn't anywhere near the top 10, and I wanted to be one of the best in the world.

One year later I was in South Africa at a small-wave event called the Mr. Price Pro in Durban for the WQS, and after that day's contest, a group of us surfed at a stationary wave park in a shopping mall, called a "flow rider." It was so fun, but on the last day before my flight, I got flipped upside down at a weird angle, and I landed hard on the big toe of my right foot. I was pretty sure I'd broken my toe. But I just tried to walk it off.

Two weeks later I was at the U.S. Open in Huntington Beach, California. I hadn't seen anyone about my toe, and it really, really hurt. I could still surf, but it felt a bit ginger.

I surfed my heat anyway, and when the waves are small, you've really got to use your toes and work very hard because you are grinding through nothingness, using everything you can to keep moving. And with that toe, I got knocked out in the first round.

That wasn't the first time it had happened that year. Even though I'd been surfing on the WQS Tour for three years, I just wasn't surfing my best anymore. But I had too much ego to listen to my intuition.

At least my toe made me listen to my body. I saw a physiotherapist at the event, and he confirmed my suspicion. The broken toe meant that I would be out of the next leg of competitions, which would include all the events in England, France, and Spain.

Standing there in the medical tent, feeling a bit sorry for myself, I was processing that my season was over when I remembered a moment a year ago, while I was competing in France. The waves were tiny. Instead of being excited and hoping the event would still go on, I'd hoped they would call it off—and they did. I'd had a moment of clarity that day. I'd realized I wasn't passionate about small waves and shouldn't be doing this because my heart wasn't in it any longer.

But I *still* didn't listen to myself. I pushed that thought aside and continued to compete in small-wave competitions for the next year. I was so determined to achieve what I'd set out to. I was stubborn and refused to give up the goal I'd set.

But then there I was in the medical tent, *a year later.* It was a moment of realization: *Shit, I've been bashing my head against a wall for almost a year now.*

I'd been going through the motions for an entire year, but I hadn't gotten the message.

On the plane from the U.S. Open in Los Angeles back home to Australia, I admitted to myself that even if my toe wasn't broken, I shouldn't be going to Europe anyway. I didn't feel excited; I felt drained just thinking about going through that tour again.

I was in a window seat, and I had plenty of time to stare at the clouds and reflect on what to do next over the 14-hour flight. At some point I decided that trying to continue to chase the small-wave tour wasn't my dream anymore.

As I had grown more and more frustrated over the past year, I had turned my attention to weight and cardio training. Honestly, it didn't make sense for a small-wave guy to be training. A part of my subconscious mind just wanted to be really fit and really strong. I didn't really understand why I felt so driven to train that way; I just did.

Back on that flight, I was thinking, *If I know I don't like this, then what do I like, whether I am paid to do it or not?* It didn't feel like I was flowing when I surfed small, weak waves. I was a heavier guy, and I just didn't like standing up, trying one turn, and then having the wave be over. On the other hand, if I could get a little wave and it ran for a while, it was superfun. But where the WQS events were, we were on tiny beach breaks in France or in England on a crappy closeout beach. The waves were pathetic, and I didn't enjoy surfing pathetic waves. I was supposed to be living it, breathing it, and loving it. I didn't have the ability then to look at my surfing and ask myself, "Can I surf these little waves and be competitive? Can I redefine my talents as a surfer and realign myself to do what is competitive in this environment?"

If I could go and do just what I wanted, what would that be?

Instantly the thought of big waves lit me up with energy. It made sense because subconsciously I had been doing it for so long without really even knowing. If I just surfed big waves, then all that training would now be relevant, because I would actually need a really strong neck and body to handle what the ocean dishes out.

I decided to let small-wave surfing go and only do big-wave trips and bigger-wave contests like Pipeline in Hawaii and Teahupo'o in Tahiti.

Back home, with a new passion in my heart and a new direction in my head, I decided to call my major sponsor and tell him that I really appreciated the support but that I was not going to keep doing the WQS. I was going to tell him my heart was no longer in it. I knew he would probably not want to sponsor me anymore, and that was okay. I was thinking about how I was going to word it, and I was nervous about telling him, but I knew I had to bite the bullet.

CASE STUDY: THANKYOU (WWW.THANKYOU.CO)
This brand began in 2008 in response to the World Water Crisis. Co-founder Daniel Flynn and friends launched a line of bottled water that would fund water projects overseas. They now have over 40 products available, and they donate 100 percent of their profits to fund safe water, food, and hygiene and sanitation services around the world.

WHEN FATE INTERVENES ON YOUR BEHALF

The day before I was going to call my sponsor, I got a call from the C.E.O. of that company, Michael Heath of Pacific Brands. Pacific Brands owned a chain of about five different clothing lines, many of which I wore. Michael said, "Just quickly, I know you like doing the competition surfing, but what are your thoughts on just surfing big waves?"

Totally caught off guard, I said, "What?" I was thinking, *Is he taking the piss out of me, or has someone told him that I was thinking this?* But I hadn't really talked about this with anyone. I kept quiet and listened.

He said, "This brand's heritage comes from Pipeline, and the brand is all about Pipeline in Hawaii, which is a big, barreling wave. Its slogan is 'Hell or High Water,' and we've been seeing so many photos of you on bigger waves. If you're interested, we would rather you focus the whole year on doing that and giving us more of these big-wave images so we can use that in our marketing."

My mouth was probably hanging wide-open at this point.

I'd been thinking about throwing my career away because I'd realized I was in the wrong area, and I was prepared to tell this guy that I quit. And then he rings and tells me that he wants the company to go in the same direction as my new dream!

Of course I stepped right up. "Yes, yes!" I responded, still in shock. And that was all it took to start my big-wave career.

Toward the end of the conversation, as I was coming down from my adrenaline rush, he said, "By the way, we'll pay you way more to do this because you are going to have to spend more time traveling and training."

Seriously, could it get any better?

In the span of one phone call, my fears were put to rest, my new direction was affirmed, and my new three-year contract increased by nearly 75 percent. All because I was willing to let go of something that no longer served me.

MIRROR THE BEST TO BECOME THE BEST

After leaving the small-wave scene, I knew that I was going to be able to chase big swells, and I knew becoming a big-wave surfer was the path I wanted to go down. But in the core world of surfing, you can't just say that and make it magically true. You have to have the runs on the board, have it clearly documented and publicized by magazines, and have a big-name company as your sponsor plastering it everywhere for your peers to see.

I didn't have any of that. I was the quiet kid who never hung out with the hard-core madmen. I didn't have the huge surf brand sponsor marketing push behind me. I didn't personally know any of the who's whos of my sport. But I had to declare it and own the space that I wanted to be in, *even though I wasn't actually there yet.*

I knew that I had to live it, feel it, and act how I wanted to be in every way to actually become it. That's not to say I was delusional and thought I was the best. I knew I was learning and growing. But I had to identify *who I was to become.* It is the same as speaking your intentions into existence. Declare a thing—and keep declaring it—and it will happen if you take action.

I truly believed deep down that I could ride the biggest waves in the world. I didn't feel that I needed to stop and wait for someone else's approval to go and live my life, doing what I dreamed of doing. When you think about it, it sounds ridiculous to think that anyone would hold back from doing what their heart desires just because someone else doesn't think it's worthwhile. But it happens all the time.

It is our life. We should all do what we love doing.

I was heavily scrutinized for saying, "I'm now a big-wave surfer," without any official accolades or results to prove it. People used to have to surf big waves for ages before they could say they were big-wave surfers.

In Australia people are very quiet about their business, and you keep doing what you're doing. If someone says to you, "Well done," the response is often to say thanks but not say anything else about it, or even to deflect compliments altogether. So for someone to be talking about what he wanted to do, like I was, it really went against the grain. And honestly that's the approach I would have liked to take—that way, there wouldn't have been pressure. If you fail, no one will hold you accountable, especially if they don't know what your goal was to begin with. But if you stand up and say what you are going to do, you're under serious pressure—both from yourself and from those you've shared your goals with—to follow through.

Anyway, I didn't have a choice. My sponsors were paying me, telling me their marketing plans, and wanting me to be this big-wave surfer. They forced me to step up. I'm not sure I would have had the drive to push myself without that and would have just sat quietly in the shadows doing whatever was easy.

When I said I was a big-wave surfer, I was written off by many. I had chosen to put myself out there, but I was actually a pretty shy person and vulnerable to criticism. When I was out surfing or would bump into someone I knew, I would sometimes be worried that they would ask me what I was up to. Because I'd have two choices: lie or tell the truth and wait for their response.

It hurt to see the look on someone's face if they laughed at me or thought that my chosen path was silly. Mind you, not everyone had a negative reaction. Some people were stoked. But others doubted my ability to be a big-wave surfer, and it was hard not to take that personally on some level. However, those experiences became a really important lesson for me, because no matter what anyone else said, I had to be totally proud, totally solid, and totally committed to the choice of what I wanted to do. I had to believe in myself as an individual 100 percent and truly know, without a shadow of doubt, that I could do this!

GOING WITH THE GRAIN

As soon as I made the switch, everything became really easy. It may sound far-fetched to think that the universe can open up to your dreams, but opportunities started coming out of the woodwork. I had offers to go places to meet up with other big-wave guys and have them teach and train me. I jumped at the chances I was given and continued my training.

When I decided to train hard (both in the gym and on the waves) and give it everything, it was a natural fit. I was fresh and new to the scene, and I was pumped! I was putting more effort in and going to more swells than a lot of the other guys, who stayed in one location and didn't travel around.

Within my first year, I was runner-up in the Big Wave Awards. That was a massive jump and a huge step in the right direction. All the energy was flowing together and happening with ease because I had the passion. Although it was still hard work, it didn't *feel like* hard work.

When I made the change and was in a position to win, a lot of people downplayed my worth. They'd say, "He just came off the small-wave circus [the WQS Tour]." I had to earn my right to be acknowledged by just doing my time. I had gone from three years of doing the grind in the WQS and finishing 64th in a handful of events—and thinking that was a good result—to finishing the year as a finalist in the Big Wave Awards!

I was putting in a load of work, but because I had so much passion, it felt like I was plugged into an internal power source. I wasn't waking up feeling burned-out. I was waking up excited to do it all over again.

Likewise, when you're in the flow of your Big Wave, you'll feel a renewed sense of passion in your life. Everything will feel right, make sense, and come fast and easy. The energy you put into it comes back to you tenfold. It not only gives you new life; it also splashes over to those around you, giving them a burst of energy and confidence too.

When you're living your passion, you can't help but be a more loving, happier person. You'll sleep more soundly and have a more positive outlook on the world in general, despite the daily chaos around you. You'll form closer bonds with your partner, your friends, and your family because you won't be spending so much time stressed out and unhappy.

If ever you're feeling drained, depressed, upset, or like a victim, you can guarantee that somewhere in your life, your flow has been disrupted. If I'm not surfing well or training well, I can recognize it and then work to regain my focus and realign my behavior with my goals. While you can't control how other people act, you can control how you react to what life throws your way. With a little practice you can learn to isolate any negative feelings and devise a path around the obstacles that are keeping you from going with the grain.

THERE IS NO APPROVAL TICKET

My family was supportive, but none of them were superstar athletes. And none of my best friends were, either, so I didn't have many role models to look up to when it came to doing something out of the box. My parents were more practical. And although they certainly wanted the best for me, even they had on blinders when it came to my possibilities.

When I was a teenager and had really gotten into surfing, my dad said he thought I should go and learn a trade and work as an apprentice instead of trying to become a professional surfer. He acknowledged that I had talent, but he wasn't able to see that I could be successful doing it.

Even outside influences were working against me. We lived in an area where there were only small waves. In the surfing world, anyone who is not from a spot where big waves are, it's often thought that they are not going to have a space in big-wave surfing. Now is that the truth? Absolutely not. But it's one more barrier that can crush your thinking before you even try.

If I'd listened to my dad or to what other people said instead of my own gut, I might be doing construction today instead of surfing all over the world. Both of those jobs are equally valuable, but one of them would be life-giving to me, and one would not.

Following a Big Wave is about proving something to *yourself*, not others. Sure, a little ego, at least at the outset, is okay. Sometimes you're the only person who can infuse positive reinforcement into your own dreams. But if it becomes all about showing off and being *better than* others, instead of being the best you can be, you're sure to come crashing down from your pedestal sooner or later.

What if you're not sure about your true intentions? Some of us have an internal hang-up when it comes to pride. So let me set this straight: having pride over your accomplishments is not a bad thing. Feeling immense happiness for attaining your goals isn't a bad thing. These are positive emotions, necessary responses if you're going to continue to make progress. The negative repercussions come when you experience happiness and, at the same time, feel as though you're better than someone else, look down on others, use your position to control others, or are happy that someone else didn't accomplish their goal.

In the spirit of good sportsmanship—even if your Big Wave isn't sports-related—it is absolutely possible to achieve your dreams, feel pride in your accomplishments, and still be humble. One of the best ways to encourage other people is by helping them along as they work to achieve their own dreams. Sometimes a kind word is all it takes to help someone move a few steps forward.

Let's say you don't have external approval. What does it take to succeed? Not all of us are lucky enough to have the support of family, friends, or co-workers. Sometimes you're the only person who believes in your dream. And sometimes, depending on the situation, you have to keep it hidden, being careful not to share it with those who will be quick to discredit your goal—or you. In those instances, you have to manifest your own encouragement. The good news is that it can be done!

Here are some healthy ways to encourage yourself when you're walking this portion of your path alone:

1. Positive affirmations: This is about *you* speaking positive thoughts for yourself. Find several of your favorite inspirational quotes or verses, and put them around your room, your house, and in your car where you can see them daily. Repeat them *out loud* to yourself. If it feels silly, who cares? Just trust me on this. Do it for a few days and you'll begin to feel a shift in your core.

2. Prayer or meditation: Make time to read sacred material, pray, or meditate every day. Even five minutes of uninterrupted silence can reduce stress, focus you on the goal at hand, and reinforce your determination that your goal is worthwhile and you are worthy of it.

3. Move your body: Whether you do yoga, jog a mile every morning, or walk around the block after dinner, moving your body in some way each day is a great way to collect your thoughts and settle anxiety.

4. Use food as fuel: I'm not going to ask you to stick to a particular diet or eating style to achieve your goals, but you should know by now which foods give you sustained energy and which make you feel like crap. Eating clean, unprocessed foods is great for all aspects of your health, including clear thinking, fewer cravings and sugar spikes, and better sleep.

When it comes down to it, you are in charge of your dream, and you're in charge of the means by which you achieve it. If it feels like a burden to be responsible for so much—shift your thinking instead to this: It's a gift to have the opportunity to reach your goal, and it's a privilege to be able to do so under your own power. You can design your life however you want. Start small and go from there.

NO REGRETS

I don't know about you, but I don't want to be 80 years old and look back and think, *I had all these awesome ideas but no willpower to try them out.* I don't want to have these dreams go unfulfilled and one day tell my kids about my ideas of *what could have been* because I never followed through. That's not an ego issue, either. It's a teachable lesson for the generations coming up behind you. Just think of what kind of example that would set for my kids and grandkids if I had all these stories of *what I wished I would have done,* and nothing to show for it. It would teach them to dream big but never take any action!

Likewise, what kind of positive example could you set for your own family and your community? Who else could you inspire in your life? What other opportunities could arise because you took the risk to step out in preparation for your Big Wave?

I knew I wanted to be able to say I put in everything I could—I left no stone unturned. I knew going in that I might hear criticism, both from people who were close to me and from my peers—and I did. It would also mean I might fail now and again—and I did. After all, failing a few times (or a hundred times) doesn't mean you have failed permanently! You only truly fail if you give up and stop learning.

I knew what it looked like to have a dream ruined. One of my friends growing up was a talented athlete and one of the most determined football players I'd ever seen. He had the height, speed—everything—and he was just amazing at what he did. He started to get scholarships to go into the AFL, which is a big deal because AFL players often get drafted for other professional sports teams. He was about to be given the golden ticket, but he got caught up in the world of drugs, and he lost any chance he had of reaching his full athletic ability. His battle with drugs pulled his family apart and ruined his life and his mind. I had never seen such a talented person's gift go to waste, which made me even more determined to follow through with my dream.

There are other examples we've all heard of people saying they really wanted to do this hobby or that activity, but instead they take or keep a safe job so they have a guaranteed income. When they get close to retirement age, they think, *I really wish I had pursued what I wanted to do*, and they end up bitter. In the end, "playing it safe" is not necessarily all that safe, because even if you've had an impressive career and a guaranteed income, you could still end up miserable and disappointed because you didn't follow your passion.

Of course you need money to live. You need the safety of home and basic necessities, but that's not what I'm talking about here. Every day we're surrounded by hundreds, if not thousands, of people who have given up a dream because it is easier to play it safe. It might only take submitting an application for a different job. It might take saving up enough money to quit your current job. It might require you to get up 30 minutes earlier every day so you can run or meditate or finish that business plan. It might mean letting go of that toxic relationship so you can freely pursue your goals.

In the end there's risk in playing it safe, and there is risk in going after your dreams. You must choose one. And in my opinion, playing it safe often causes deep regret down the road.

We both know you deserve better than that.

EXERCISE: WHAT'S STOPPING YOU FROM GOING AFTER YOUR BIG WAVE?

You can't trick people into taking risks, but you can convince them of the benefits! So we're going to do a worst-case scenario, best-case scenario exercise that will help you work through your fears and see that quite often, the worst-case scenario—the one that most often keeps us stuck—is the least likely outcome of your situation.

Fill in the blanks below and keep going until you've exhausted all the fears you have.

(Example)
My Big Wave is to run a full marathon.
First action: Entering the race.
Worst-case scenario: I've just spent $80 on something I'm not sure I can do.
Best-case scenario: I've just entered my first full marathon! What an awesome experience! I can do this.

Next action: Set up a training schedule.
Worst-case scenario: I have to get up at 5:30 every morning and run.
Best-case scenario: It's guaranteed exercise every day, and I'll build endurance. I'll also have more energy the rest of the day.

Next action: Join a running group for accountability.

Worst-case scenario: I won't like the people, or they'll be faster than me.

Best-case scenario: I'll make some awesome friends, and I bet some of them are also beginners.

My Big Wave is

_____

First action:

_____

Worst-case scenario:

_____

_____

Best-case scenario:

_____

_____

Next action:

_____

Worst-case scenario:

_____

_____

Best-case scenario:

_____

_____

Next action:

_____

Worst-case scenario:

_____

_____

Best-case scenario:

_____

_____

CHAPTER 3

STEP #1:
GIVE UP THE STORY

If you're trying to achieve, there will be roadblocks. I've had them; everybody has had them. But obstacles don't have to stop you. If you run into a wall, don't turn around and give up. Figure out how to climb it, go through it, or work around it.

— MICHAEL JORDAN

In the start of 2000, when I was about 17 years old, my surfing coach, Porto, told me and my friends about a contest at Burleigh Heads on the Gold Coast, which was about a two-hour drive south from our place. We were excited to go but had no idea where we would stay for the weekend. Luckily Porto said to me, "You and my son can go and stay at a friend's house for this contest. She isn't there, but I'll tell you where the key is so you can go and leave all your boards there." It just so happened that the house was right in front of where that contest was going to be. My coach's son and I stayed at this house and had a great time at the event.

Something that stood out about the house, apart from its awesome construction, was that there were little notes all over the place: in the kitchen, in the bathroom, on the walls, and even some on the doors. I made sure not to bump any of them or knock them off the walls. The house was massive—three stories high with a gym and a rope from the balcony to the ground for a fitness and training regimen. But what stuck out most in my mind was that it was strange to have notes taped all around.

About a week later, I was down on the Gold Coast picking up a few new boards, and I thought since I was at that end of town, I would pop by the house again and thank the owner for letting us stay there for free.

I pulled into the driveway, knocked on the door, introduced myself to the man who answered, and thanked him.

Apparently the man's ex-wife was the owner and no longer lived there. He, Steve White, had no idea who I was, but he knew Porto, and he knew we'd stayed at his home. He said, "If you ever want to stay ever again, you are more than welcome to." Such a nice offer from someone I had only just met! The massive house was right across the street from the ocean, and there was plenty of space to keep surfboards. When you're 17 years old, and someone allows you to stay at a mansion on the beach, you'd have to be mad to turn that down.

Several weeks later I was down on the Gold Coast again, and I had just picked up 10 boards. When you compete on the surfing tour, you need three or four boards the exact same size. Since they're so light, you go through so many of them because they break easily. And if you went to Western Australia, Hawaii, or Tahiti, you might easily break 10 boards in one trip. I used to go through an average of 27 boards in a year, and compared with other surfers, I didn't even go through that many.

I wanted to put my boards somewhere while I went surfing for a couple of hours so if my car got broken into they wouldn't get stolen. Then I remembered Steve White.

This time when I visited, he walked me around the house. As we went from room to room, I noticed even more notes—pieces of paper taped above light switches and on door frames and above clocks. Some were words and phrases; others were numbers that looked like codes. I was intrigued, and I couldn't help wondering, *Who is this guy? This dude's a proper weirdo.*

As we walked around the rooms, I began to notice more about Steve than I had before. He was in his mid-40s, but he was the most superior human I had ever seen. Even with all the athletes I hung out with day after day, I had never seen someone so fit and healthy and happy in my life. He was so positive and took full responsibility for everything without an ego. I thought, *This guy is on to something. He has all these codes everywhere, he looks amazingly fit, and he's the nicest guy ever. What's his secret?*

I knew he surfed and saw it as a fun and healthy sport, but he didn't compete in events. His former wife was a keen surfer who had won numerous Queensland and Australian Malibu surfing titles. Because he was well aware of the lifestyle I was leading and I felt like we got along really well, it was easy to talk to him about anything.

I told him how I had this internal desire to become more, to become extraordinary, though I didn't know what that really meant at the time. These were grandiose dreams coming from a 17-year-old, but Steve listened and never shut me down or discouraged me.

He seemed like a supernice guy. But I was still very curious about the notes. So I asked him what it all meant.

As soon as I spoke, he got a look in his eye like he'd heard that question before. Maybe he thought I was looking for a shortcut in life. Sensing his hesitation, I said, "I am really keen to learn."

Taking the bait, he said he'd give me some audio recordings of a series by a guy named Brian Tracy, called "The Psychology of Achievement." He said, "I want you to listen to these, and once you've listened to them, give me a call. Then I will start to fill you in on what everything means and how it all works."

So I took the collection, went home, and listened to it over and over again, writing down all the lessons and thoughts I had learned from it. There were sections on time management, accepting compliments, the Law of Attraction, and postural behavior, and I wrote a page or more of notes in great detail, including all the key points and how I could apply them to my life. I went back a week or two later and told Steve about it, and that's really how my true education began.

He would feed me information a small amount at a time, and I would take in what I could. Then he would give me the next thing, and I would absorb it like a dry sponge. He was also quick to point out areas where he believed I was holding myself back.

STORIES AND BELIEFS

Over the course of several months, he continued to say to me, "Give up the story."

I never knew what that meant. I'd respond, "What story?"

He'd say, "Oh, you keep telling yourself this story of why you can't do what you say you want to do," and it was frustrating, because I didn't understand what that actually meant—at first.

The material I was learning, along with his coaching, literally changed the way I thought. With his help, I was able to recognize and isolate the self-defeating thoughts, stories, and beliefs I'd carried with me from childhood—thoughts that I wasn't good enough or that I didn't deserve any type of success.

These stories applied to every area of my life, and they were most evident in surfing. I was able to realize the story—the excuses for why I couldn't do what I said I wanted to do—in the reasons that I got knocked out of a surfing contest. My first excuse would have been because my surfboard wasn't really working out there in those conditions. In surfing competitions, you can win one week and get knocked out the next. You are dealing with nature, and you can't predict when a wave will or won't come. But that was just an excuse, and I was never really taking responsibility for myself. I never fully admitted to myself that I just didn't have it together, or that I didn't put in the work beforehand as hard as I needed to, or that I was working on the wrong areas.

There are just so many excuses we tell ourselves. What Steve was trying to make me do was take ownership of it and accept it for what it was. It was hard. But I was slowly getting it.

I learned more and more about Steve, as well. He'd come out of a professional league on a National Rugby League (NRL) team called the Canterbury Bulldogs, which is the highest level of professional Rugby League football in Australia. While part of that team, he had been involved in hypnosis and learned about the power of the mind. He had a black belt in several martial arts. He had also attended a lot of personal-growth seminars over the years, including completion of Tony Robbins's Mastery University. At the time we met, Steve was helping several world-class athletes get exposure to this material to enhance their mental capacity and strength.

As we reviewed the latest material I'd listened to, he said, "Your mind is like a playlist. You can skip around and listen to different tracks, but eventually you will listen to all the same songs." I looked at him with some confusion. So he clarified: "You need to be able to change your whole playlist, not just skip over tracks."

"How do you do that?" I asked.

He said, "Remember when you asked me about all these little things above the lights, the clocks, and on the fridge?" Of course I did. He then explained that they were reminders to change habits. Every time he saw a note in his house, it referred to something he was working on, whether it was his posture or adjusting his train of thought. These notes constantly reminded him to think about a certain thing, and they were how he reprogrammed his mind to think and feel the way he wanted to feel. A sticker that read "P" on a door frame might have meant to check his posture. Another sticker read, "Thought Pattern," and another read, "Feel Good."

It had obviously worked for him, and since he was so generous in passing this information on to me, I decided to try it out. I put stickers on my car keys and light switches to remind me of specific things I wanted to work on, such as my posture and my self-limiting beliefs. All my friends thought I was a weirdo, but I didn't care. I'd seen the benefits in Steve's life, and I wanted the same benefits. If I could work on all these issues and I got to end up like Steve one day, that's what I wanted.

My codes and messages were different than his; each person has a unique background and experiences that create their self-limiting beliefs. I was also starting from scratch. But there were certain things he pointed out to me as he got to know me better. My initial focus was on being aware of my body and my mind, and making subtle shifts when necessary.

Once he started to realize what my normal thought patterns were, he asked me a series of questions to see how I'd respond. Then he'd ask me how I would want to think instead, or what my ideal outcomes were. The codes and messages I'd create for myself and then choose to place around my house and environment would be a reminder of my specific desires to change.

GIVING UP THE STORY FOR GOOD

While posture, time management, and being able to avoid deflecting compliments given to me seemed like beneficial things to work on, the harder one was giving up the story I'd been telling myself since I was a child—that I wasn't good enough or worthy enough to achieve anything great.

In a few places in my house, including a memo permanently saved on my phone, a note under my light switch in my bedroom, another piece of paper taped to my clock, and a small reminder on my car keys, I wrote, "Give up the story." Several months into this self-work, I'd discovered that I always had a story—an excuse—whether I realized it or not. *I can't do* that *because of* this. It must have been a thing that I taught myself to do at a young age, maybe so I wouldn't get my hopes up and be disappointed. This disbelief in myself had permeated every layer of my life in some way.

It took around nine months of continually having to check myself and correct myself before I began to see real changes in my life, like better posture, more confidence, more positive and welcoming responses to compliments, and a better overall attitude.

I know we all wish changes like this could be made overnight by reciting the right words and filing a list away in a journal somewhere. But, like Steve said, such minimal effort would be the equivalent to just changing audio tracks. And then over a period of about a month, you would go back into an old habit.

He'd told me when we began that it would take at least six months to see progress. Like I mentioned, I've always been a bit stubborn, so perhaps that's why it took me a little longer. I remember in those first few months, I would say to myself, "Shit, six months is a really long time!" But I'd quickly remind myself of the goal: Would I sacrifice this many months right now to never have to feel stuck in that old pattern of living and thinking again, for the rest of my life? Each and every time, the answer was "Absolutely."

When I was starting to surf, and even when I'd begun to win events and awards, I was still filled with doubt. My stories about myself and my worth directly affected my actions. I believed that I didn't have a real chance to be a champion surfer because I came from a farming area away from the ocean. I didn't believe I was anything other than average, so I was surfing in an average way.

At the time when my confidence and belief system were forming, the doubts became embedded in my mental tracks and kept playing in the background, even when I wasn't aware of them.

To make changes in your own life, you've got to first discover your faulty stories, and then you have to reprogram your stories.

Maybe you've had the same thought I did: *Gosh, I don't have a great story. I wasn't born with a silver spoon in my mouth. Nor was I born into great adversity and have a seemingly innate drive to overcome my circumstances.* Maybe you're married with kids. Maybe you're 30 years into your career and feel like you have to live a normal life, whatever that means to you. The truth is you can do whatever you want. It's all in your head. Whatever stories you are making up, it's all just complete bullshit. There is no right or wrong. If you want anything, you can do whatever you want.

I had all these reasons to try to justify what wouldn't allow me to work toward my dream, but once I dropped the bullshit stories, I saw that I was the only one standing in my way. Likewise, as soon as you allow yourself to drop the stories, you can do whatever you want.

CASE STUDY: TOMS (WWW.TOMS.COM)
Blake Mycoskie, a serial entrepreneur from Texas, saw a need for shoes while traveling in Argentina and started Toms with a one-for-one business plan. For every pair of shoes purchased, another pair is donated to a child in need. They've now given more than 60 million pairs of shoes to children in need.

Below, make a list of all the excuses and stories you've told yourself (or that other people have told you about yourself) that are getting in the way of your dream. It doesn't matter how small or far-fetched they sound; every story you've told yourself has taken root in some way in your patterns of thinking.

I can't achieve my dream because:

1. _____

   _____

2. _____

   _____

3. _____

   _____

4. _____

   _____

5. _____

   _____

6. _____

   _____

List other excuses and stories that family and friends may have told you about your dream:

1. _____

_____

2. _____

_____

3. _____

_____

4. _____

_____

5. _____

_____

6. _____

_____

I had to change the way I looked at things if I wanted to change my present-day life and my future. I didn't need someone else to tell me I was the best or that I was worthy; I needed to believe it myself.

TAKING PERSONAL RESPONSIBILITY

When you've done the work of really looking at your dreams and fears, you'll likely see that yes—your Big Wave is not only possible but plausible. You are just the right person to do it. What's left is to take personal responsibility and make it happen.

Steve mentioned several times that I needed to take personal responsibility for everything that happened in my life—*everything*. He would tell me things like, "If you are driving around on a road, where all the other cars are driving way too fast, and one of those guys crashes into you, that's your fault."

I thought he was crazy to say a car crash caused by someone else was my responsibility. "How is that my fault? Someone else crashed into me."

He said, "You chose to put yourself in that situation."

It didn't make sense at the time, but once I understood that I did indeed have control over my circumstances—including Steve's example of making the choice to get into a car, which provided the opportunity for another driver to hit my car—I had an epiphany. I was responsible for every situation I was in, because every situation represented a choice I had made. That put a lot of pressure on me and my choices in a way, but it was also freeing. Being responsible for every choice meant being responsible for the good ones too, not just the bad. And acknowledging that you're responsible for your choices makes you want to make good ones!

One summer when I was surfing a wave down the coast with some friends, I told them that I heard the water could be cold at that time of year based on different currents. My friends looked at me like I was joking and reminded me that it was always warm this time of year, since it was summer. All the other guys packed board shorts, and I remember thinking that I could do what everyone else was doing to be cool, or since there was a chance that the water could be cold, I could pack a full-length wetsuit.

All the guys laughed at me for carrying the extra backpack, but when we got to the spot, the water was freezing. I was the only one in my group who had a full suit. The other guys complained I was lucky and they were unlucky for not bringing theirs, but at the end of the day, we'd each had a choice. I had taken the responsibility for myself and because of that, I got to surf and my friends could only last 10 minutes before they froze up!

When you take ownership of everything, it changes your outlook on why things are a certain way, and what you need to do to have different results. Taking responsibility for everything in your life means being fully prepared for all situations. Professional athletes, C.E.O.s, businesspeople, parents, and students alike who have that attribute are always ready for anything—they are the ones who always end up on top. Nothing happens by chance with those people. They live intentional lives. And while they can't predict everything that will happen, they, like my mentor Steve, have prepared themselves to react to any circumstance.

As a result of taking ownership of anything that didn't go the way I wanted it to, from a straightforward, young-minded point of view, I was just like, "Okay, well, if that happens, then I need to prepare for that." That sense of personal responsibility made me put in extra work in order to stop any mistakes happening again. So, for example, if I kept falling off my board in a certain way, it would indicate an error in technique. Instead of just accepting that I wasn't that good a surfer, I would go work on that technique.

After my mentorship with Steve and my epiphany, when a problem came up, instead of making an excuse like I'd done for years, I'd ask myself, "How can I look at that exact situation and then change it, train for it, or overcome it?" Then another obstacle would come, but by taking ownership of it and taking responsibility for it, I accepted it and learned how to move around it, go over it, or go to the side of it. It was almost like roadblocks didn't actually exist—they were just something I needed to train for.

It made me bulletproof in a way, because now I was prepared for all these things.

I also had a really wild daydream experience that gave me a different perspective on my life. Steve had worked with hypnotherapy and thought highly of it, so when I was 21, I went to see a local hypnotherapist. She told me, "Your life has already been written out for you, and you're just living it."

I thought, *This is bullshit!* And I said to her, "Can you tell the people who wrote my script to change it?" I didn't want to be a normal person and live a normal life. I wanted to live the life that appeared when I closed my eyes and dreamed.

I'm quite sure she had a better understanding of things than I did as a 21-year-old. She said, "Just close your eyes and count backward." Soon I was in a daydream. She was still talking to me, saying, "That's right. You've been here before."

In my mind I was surfing this massive wave, Teahupo'o in Tahiti. At the time, that was one of the scariest waves I'd ever heard of, and I hadn't surfed it yet. I thought she was full of shit because she was saying I'd been there, but I knew I hadn't.

Then I started to visualize surfing, and every time I did a turn or a maneuver, water would fly up into the sky and turn a gold color. The most spectacular spray of gold would fly into the air, almost as if someone had thrown a handful of gold dust over me.

After the wave, I shook my head to get the water off me and out of my face, and I realized my hair was like a lion's mane and where I shook my hair, all the water that came off me was gold. In that moment, it was a strong realization that being in the water was like gold for me. It was the place I belonged, where I had a great deal of wealth.

As weird as that experience was, I left with a sense of peace that I was on the right track. Not only that, but after Steve's guidance, I was now *very aware* that I needed to take responsibility for my own life and my dreams.

When you accept that you are responsible for everything in your life, at first it may seem like a lot to take ownership of, but personal responsibility shows up in our lives in many ways. The benefits of taking full personal responsibility include feeling a lot more empowered and confident, and making better decisions as you begin to understand how each decision really does matter.

The opposite of personal responsibility is the victim mind-set, where a person will deny that they're responsible for anything in life and feel unable to control the bad things that have happened to them, so they get stuck in an uncomfortable life.

Unfortunate things—even terrible things—often happen to good people, and there's often no explanation. I'm not saying that you are responsible for *causing* anything bad that has happened to you, any trauma that has come your way, or any illnesses. What I am saying is that even in the midst of pain, in the midst of sadness, and in the midst of illness, as long as you still have breath in your body, you still have the ability to change your mind-set, your reactions, and your future.

It's time to let go of those old stories so you can fully embrace the new one you're in the midst of creating. Your golden moment might be right around the corner.

CHAPTER 4

STEP #2:
FIND YOUR LINE

All successful people are big dreamers.
They imagine what their future could be, ideal in
every respect, and then they work every day toward
their distant vision, that goal or purpose.

— BRIAN TRACY

When you are riding a big wave, you have to find your line, which means choosing your path. "The line" or "the path" that you are going to take on the wave determines whether you will catch a rail and wipe out, or ride it in the most stylish or effortless way possible. In some ways, it's very similar to snowboarding or skiing, in that there's space in front of you and you get to choose how to approach it, carving your own path into the surface ahead.

When I ride a big wave, I think about my plan of approach constantly: "I'm going to go up high, and then I'm going to carve down here, and then I'm going to bottom turn there." With any dream, once you're about to take action, you are picking the lines you are going to take, making sure you have an exit point, and brainstorming the ways you might have to deal with a situation that could unfold in front of you.

So when you see a big wave wrapping around the corner, pick your path, the line you are going to take, and then get busy executing it.

MAKING THE SHIFT

It might seem like my shift from small-wave surfing to big waves was effortless—I made a decision, my sponsor called with news, and things miraculously fell into place. But there was quite a bit of preparation that had to go into that shift once the phone call was over.

First of all, with each new dream or new path, there are new and different obstacles to consider. I now had to identify all the obstacles I would have to overcome. One of the obvious changes was in my training. If I was going to focus fully on big-wave surfing, I didn't need to do the small-wave training workouts anymore, which included fast-paddling drills and explosive body movements to replicate the speed needed to make sharp turns on a small wave. Instead I needed to get to work on some big-wave training, and that required me to have a much stronger neck, core, and legs to sustain me in a wipeout. I needed greater endurance as a swimmer and in holding my breath underwater. I also needed to run paddle drills on much larger boards.

In addition to the physical training, I needed to think about the external obstacles that could get in my way of wanting to be a big-wave surfer. What could stop me on my path?

First, I could drown. I could basically get snapped in half.

I knew I needed to focus on the anxiety of being out of control, so I needed to try to eliminate that as much as possible through relaxation and taking control of my thoughts.

CASE STUDY: POLO RALPH LAUREN (WWW.RALPHLAUREN.COM)
While working at Brooks Brothers, Ralph Lauren began designing his own line of men's neckties in 1967, and several years later he was awarded for his designs. Today Lauren is an iconic American fashion designer and business executive, and the Polo Ralph Lauren Foundation supports initiatives in cancer care, education, and service in underserved communities. As of May 2016, nearly 50 years after inception, the company is worth $7.9 billion.

Another change would be that I'd have to travel to these different areas. How was I going to do that easily? Who was I going to travel with? For the most part, small-wave surfers and big-wave surfers were two totally separate groups of people, and all my travel buddies were still doing small-wave events. I was going to have to make some new friends.

I also had to deal with surfing new seasons, because winter in one country is summer in another. While the small-wave tour brought surfers together in the summers in Australia and California, the big waves were during everyone else's winter. It just happened to be winter in Australia when I first got into big waves.

I had to learn a different lifestyle, for sure. Some of the guys who were dedicated to big waves wouldn't even leave the area to surf anywhere else. They would stay in Tasmania or Hawaii and prepare for a four-month block of surfing every single swell. They would spend the rest of the year preparing for those four months of surfing. Some did also work regular day jobs. Others would go chase other countries' winters.

I needed to identify who was doing what, where they were doing it, where I could fit in with these guys, and what new skills I needed to learn. I would have to learn to drive a Jet Ski and get good at towing someone in, as well as being towed in, so I wouldn't be a waste of space. I needed to be an asset to other surfers, not a pain in their asses. I would have to put a lot of effort into being someone who could help others, as well as being comfortable asking for help.

There were so many things to consider. I basically had to look at what it was that I was going to do, be clear and open with myself about every little step, and really think about what each one was going to look like.

THE QUEST TO BE THE BEST

When I made that shift from small-wave to big-wave surfing, of course I wanted to become one of the best in the world.

Over the next year, with my broken toe healed and my new contract in place, I would travel to all the best spots. Life was about to get interesting! I paddled into Teahupo'o, Pipeline, and Waimea, and I felt like I was doing pretty great. And then in December 2006, we rocked up to Mavericks in Half Moon Bay, California, at first light. Talk about a spooky place; with a foggy haze in the sky and brownish-black water, and a constant foghorn going off, Mavericks is a tricky place to surf. The waves felt elusive. Helicopters were hovering with cameramen hanging out the sides, and I felt like I was about to go into battle.

I was running down to paddle out on a mate's borrowed 9'6", the biggest board I had ever seen at the time. As I was heading out, I could see that most of the guys were towing in on Jet Skis. That meant that the waves had to be way bigger than usual, since Mavericks is normally a paddle-in big wave. I was keen to take my tow board, as well, so I could finally get towed into a wave for the first time, so I ran back to the car and got it and my vest. I put my tow vest on and strapped the tow board to the leash of the 9'6" and started to drag it out from the rocky paddle-out point of the beach.

The water was a skin-numbing 14 degrees Celsius (57 degrees Farenheit)! I'd left my booties on the Jet Ski with the others, and that really didn't help me for the paddle out. Seals were bobbing around the shore—this place was a part of the "red triangle great white population." And I really didn't like sharks.

The tow board was becoming heavy because I was dragging it behind me, so I put the buckle of the tow vest through the board's foot straps and slung it across my back horizontally like a rifle. It was all good until I was paddling over a 10-foot shore break and the lip pitched, catching the sides of the tow board and ejecting me back over the lip. I got absolutely smashed and lost my tow board, my vest was ripped off, and I got another four sets on the head. I nearly drowned, and I hadn't even gotten past the shoreline!

By the time I got out there, I had been paddling for one hour straight, and all the boys were asking, "Where the hell have you been?" I was exhausted. Both my arms had started to cramp, as the cold water really took it out of me. Just then I saw a 30-foot set come in and thought, *Come on, arms, no time for cramping now!*

I got a few waves that day, but nothing really big. The trip was humbling, to say the least, and it left me wanting more.

MEETING JAWS FACE-TO-FACE

Two months later, in February 2007, I met Jaws for the first time. At that point I'd never put myself through so many heavy situations just to surf a wave! It was one of the toughest tests I've ever gone through.

I was at Oahu for the Pipeline WQS, and the 40-knot (46 mph) onshore winds were too strong, making the waves out of control, so the event was on hold. So I booked a flight to Maui, 116 miles away, to surf Jaws for the first time. I had no idea where to go, where I'd stay, or how I was going to do it, but I was so keen to go to Jaws.

The waves at Jaws, also known as Pe'ahi, are some of the biggest in the world. The contest had been called off at Pipeline, but Pe'ahi could handle those winds because there they wrapped in from a slightly different direction. There's one big difference between the two locations— there is no beach at Jaws, only a cliff and jagged rocks below. A big swell was coming. I'd never been towed in on a tow-in board anywhere in the world yet, and I was really eager to do it, especially after getting flattened two months earlier at Mavericks.

I knew that Jamie Sterling, another a big-wave surfer, was going to the swell for sure, so I rang him and asked him if there was any chance I could get towed in with him. His tow partner was Mark Healy, and they were frothing to go, seeing as how Jaws hadn't broken all year. He said, "Yeah, if you can get over there, get down the cliff, jump off the rocks, and paddle out. I might be able to tow you into one once we have had a few ourselves." Basically, he had just said, "I've got a plane, it's full, and you could come along, but only if you are cool with sitting on the wing." Who the hell would want to do that?

All I knew was that the cliff at Jaws was where all the totaled Jet Skis, boards, and people got smashed into, and it's the last place you ever want to end up! The boulders below the big cliff are littered with chunks of Jet Ski parts. Peter Mel (big-wave Mavericks legend) had been on my flight over, and he was telling me that he was teaming up with Ross Clark Jones (an Aussie big-wave hero of mine). He told me that the rocks were as terrible as everyone said, and that I really didn't want to be down there at all.

But it's funny. When you really want something, your mind immediately starts to break it down. How big was this cliff, anyway? How big were the boulders? Surely I could make it out if I timed it right.

Once I landed in Maui, after a few directions and a 40-minute drive in my rental car, I was standing on the cliff top of Jaws. Waves were 15 feet tall, and the wind was howling, with six tow teams out. The charts were saying the swell would be twice as big tomorrow, so a lot of guys were holding off until then. But not me. I was there and ready to give it a go!

As I walked around the cliff, I found a rope tied to a big tree at the top going all the way down a goat track to the bottom. I was watching the guys tow from the cliff and noticed two goofy-footers (which means they surf with the right foot in front and not the left, which is regular) on the left. I thought it had to be Sterls and Healy.

By then it was 4:30 in the afternoon, and I had about 90 minutes of daylight left. So I grabbed my gear and went down the cliff, board in one hand, rope in the other.

When I got to the boulders, I thought it was doable, but I'd have to paddle my tow board with the tow straps under my chest, a vest on, and no leash.

There was a cameraman filming on the bottom of the cliff, and I didn't want to stand around and talk shit or get talked out of going, so I hid in the trees until there was a break in the sets. When it came, I ran across the rocks and jumped out!

It was nearly impossible to paddle past the shore because the water was constantly sucking and thumping back into the rock. The tow vest was making it so awkward, plus trying to paddle out on a tow board is like trying to ride a kickboard—it's only 1.5 inches thick, and it just sinks underneath you. I only just made it over the shoreline. To get to the waves, I still had to paddle quite a distance from the cliff base.

Just as I was getting close to the main channel, the Jet Ski that I thought held Sterls and Healy started to drive off back toward the harbor. I was devastated! I sat out there watching, just trying to figure out what the wave does and how I thought I'd try to ride it if I got a chance the next day.

Then all of a sudden a Jet Ski came over, and this guy said, "Are you crazy, kid? You're drifting straight into the lineup." I didn't realize it, but the 40-knot offshore winds had pushed me out and over, and I was about to get the next set on the head!

Turns out it was the same guy who had seen me get a flogging at Mavericks two months earlier when I'd tried to paddle out with the tow board on my back. He leaned back and told his buddy that I was the guy that he was talking about who got hammered that day! They both started shaking their heads and laughing. Meanwhile, I was still getting pushed farther out to sea. Finally he said, "Get on the sled, Aussie. There's no way you can sit here without getting in big trouble."

They dropped me off in front of the boulders, giving me the hand signals to go toward a certain rock. I didn't move fast enough, and just as I turned around, I got swamped by a big wave that smashed me up and into the boulders, sent my tow board high and dry, and left me with a few cuts and bruises as a reminder that it was not a good idea to try that again.

As I climbed back up the goat track, hanging on to the rope, I started to doubt my chances of actually being able to get a wave at Jaws. I'd just gotten absolutely belted, and I knew it was too dangerous to be sitting on a surfboard and not being able to paddle away fast enough. The strong winds were only going to continue to push me into a bad position.

I got to the cliff top, only to see Sterling standing there with his binoculars around his neck. "Good effort, mate," he said, giving me a nod.

I said, "I don't know if I'll be able to do that again tomorrow. The guys out there said I almost drifted into the lineup, and I would have been cactus!"

Sterling said, "Well, you can go with my friend on his ski tomorrow. That will be fine!"

I thought, *That would have been great if you had told me that yesterday!* But I knew I had to earn their respect. Nothing came easy to them, so why should it for me? By going to the lengths I did, I had earned my spot on the ski for the next day. Sterls even let me stay at their place and said he'd let me use one of his tow boards made for Jaws. That night as I drifted to sleep, I was so stoked because I knew I was finally going to be able to get towed into a wave at Jaws!

The next morning we pulled up at the harbor in Maliko Bay to put the Jet Skis in. It was a 15-minute ride out to Jaws, and as we got closer, I counted 20 other Jet Skis that were already out. It was chaos!

I was watching the waves for a while, figuring it all out, and then Jamie came over and said, "You ready to go, Visser?" I was trying to get the straps for the tow board on when he gunned it. My front foot wasn't in tight, and I did the splits and ate shit. I remember the look on Sterling's face, as if he was saying, "Don't embarrass me! I'm giving you this opportunity, and you don't even know how to stand up? I hope you know what you're doing."

When you get towed into Jaws, the Jet Skis are often going 48 kilometers (about 30 miles) per hour, and you're flying through the chops, dodging other skis, trying to hang on, just to make it to the wave. If you're the driver, you've got to be aggressive. Skis bump each other to get priority and take a wave.

Sterls got me into position, but with 20 skis flying around, it was a nightmare. As I was floating, waiting to go on a wave, another ski was gunning for the same wave and he nearly ran me over! He saw me at the last second and turned to the side. I was more worried about being hit by a ski than I was about the wave.

But when I finally got a good wave, none of that mattered. I was riding an enormous wave; I had made it. I had earned it. Everything I had gone through seemed minor.

WHAT COMES NEXT?

Over the next several years, I was a runner-up in the 2008–2009, 2009–2010, and 2010–2011 Oakley ASL Big Wave Awards. I had surfed all the best big waves there were and had success at the very start.

Yet three years after making the switch, I thought, *I've been to all these places—so what else is there?*

It's kind of like having a list of theme parks you want to go to, and then once you've gone to all of them, you think, "What else do I do?" The majority of big-wave guys say you keep going back and getting better and better at every single big wave. But my imaginative mind was always thinking a few steps ahead. Now it wasn't purely ego talking, though there was certainly some ego there. But I had put in the work and training and I had been able to go surf Jaws and other big-wave spots many times, and once I had achieved those milestones, I thought, *What else could I do if I really put my mind to it?* Something big was calling me.

That's when someone approached me with an idea, and it became the project that would consume my next four years.

A guy named Crys-kai Carroll came up to me at a charity function and said, "Last night, I had the trippiest dream ever. I had this dream that you were riding this huge wave at night." He was a really nice guy who often helps people out with charity events, and at the time, he ran a local surf mag called *Sunshine Coast Surf.* I laughed, but he said, "No, it was really real that you rode this huge wave at night. My dad actually owns this company that makes headlamps for push bikes to ride at night." The company was called NiteRider, and he said I should see if I could surf with the lamps because they were fully waterproof.

He said he had used them riding small waves at night, and that if I tested it and it worked on small waves, maybe I could ride a big wave at night. I thought that it sounded crazy. So, of course, I tried it out.

I tested it the next night. Knowing that if we rode a big wave, I would have to be towed into it, we took the Jet Ski. The light shone straight forward, and it picked up all the mist. If there were chops or bumps just to the left or right of me, I wouldn't see them. I tried it several times but kept stacking it, wiping out left and right, before I was even getting close to the wave. I couldn't see the bumps and chops from the Jet Ski, and without being able to see well, I couldn't handle the speed, either. The nose of my surfboard was getting caught in the waves. It was like driving on a dark road with only one headlight and constantly hitting potholes you can't even see. We even flipped the Jet Ski trying to tow into waves as small as two feet.

Even if it had worked, the construction of the headlamp was a massive hazard. The cord was on my head, and it would wrap around my neck while I was surfing, which could easily drown me. I had been intrigued enough to give it a go, but my gut feeling was it didn't make sense. The only benefit I saw at that stage was working with Crys-kai to see if we could improve some kind of contraption for his dad's lights.

I rang him the next day and told him the results—it was dangerous and hard to do. I wasn't a big fan. I was wiping out in two-foot waves, so I didn't know how the hell you would even contemplate doing it in huge surf. I gave him his lights back and said, "Maybe if the lights were attached to the board facing backward, it might work better." I had a couple of ideas I ran by him, and he said he'd ask his dad if he would help engineer a new light.

A week later I got word that his dad straight up said no. He didn't care about allocating funds into creating lights for this particular surfing project. It sounded crazy, and he didn't see it as a worthwhile thing for him to do—which was understandable, from his point of view.

I could throw out ideas, but I was on my own. Nobody at that point was really going to help me invent something, and I was left with everything in my own court.

So I tossed the idea aside. About once a year I'd bump into Crys-kai, and he'd say, "Are you still working on that idea?"

I would go, "Oh yeah," and we'd talk about other possibilities—if you changed this or that, but I hadn't really put a large amount of energy toward it. Maybe I could make night surfing work, but every time I had a new idea for how to do it, I just went back to chasing every swell like a normal big-wave surfer did, like the person going back to all the theme parks to ride the same roller coasters. Soon I got into that routine of chasing swells everywhere. I didn't realize it until much later, but it was obvious at this point that I'd been sucked into doing or following what the other guys' goals were instead of paying attention to the feeling that it was time for me to look at something new.

THE DIFFERENCE
BETWEEN DREAMERS AND DOERS

When you want to achieve a dream, a lot of us expect it to just fall out of the sky and happen. But when we try for it, and it doesn't happen right away, and all these roadblocks come up, then there's a choice. You can either say, "Well, I didn't get my dream" and quit. Or you can look at it and say, "There are obstacles here, and I have to understand what those obstacles are, take ownership of them, learn from them, get stronger from them, and move around them."

In truth, the obstacles really just mean that you have to train harder. The mind of someone who wasn't taking responsibility would say, *Oh, this is a roadblock. This is stopping me from achieving my goal.* But when you look at it from a different point of view, you can say, "This is a skill that I haven't acquired, and I have to learn how to understand it, and as soon as I do that, I can move past it."

If you look at your life like an obstacle course, then there isn't much that can stop you. If you are prepared to go through them all, if you're expecting them, and you've trained in advance for these obstacles, you'll overcome each one and keep going.

A few years after Crys-kai Carroll told me about his dream, I ran into my friend Scott. Scott is a business guy, and when I'd bump into him, he'd ask how my surfing career was going. I was open about the fact that there is always room to grow and move. I told him that I'd been having ideas of doing something more.

By this time I had been a finalist in a few Big Wave events three years in a row, and was having success. I was traveling everywhere and getting great photos for all my sponsors. Everything was good. Everything was perfect, as far as everyone could tell. But Scott said, "You can only surf for so long."

I agreed. "Yeah, I could probably do this for 10 years, and it would be a great lifestyle." And it was true. I was only 28 years old. I knew that in my mind I was still an up-and-comer, but I still had this feeling I could push myself to a whole new level.

He asked, "What about all those other ideas that you had?"

I said, "Yeah, they are still in the pipeline."

That's when he said, "Mate, they are never going to happen unless you actually figure out how you are going to do them. If you don't work it out, they will always just be ideas or dreams."

He had a point. I hadn't lost the energy for big waves, but I had gotten to a point where I felt like I was just doing the same thing over and over. I was lacking purpose, and I was coming too much from a place of ego. I loved big waves and I had endless energy to surf them, but I got caught up in needing the results and trying to impress the sponsors and going to the biggest swells all year long. I got swept up in the ego game, and I started to forget the real reason I surfed. I needed to remember why I was doing it, or I knew I'd burn out just like I'd burned out on small waves.

So I went and talked to my friend Michael "Micky" Maidens. We had met through my manager, Steve Rafter. These days, Micky's doing a lot of amazing things in marketing and IT, launching products, helping people make an impact in the world, and really making a difference. But back then, he was just an IT guy who did computer programming and built software and a few websites. But he had a mind like a computer and was able to look at things very analytically. I knew he would be honest with me and give great advice. Plus he'd been surfing since he was 17, so we had that love in common.

Micky and I started brainstorming about what it was that I truly wanted to do and why. He was able to extract all the information and help me see the facts. He helped me figure out my core reasons for surfing—because I loved it, and because I really wanted to make an impact on myself, to prove to myself, before anyone else, that I could do this. I wanted to do something that would really challenge me as a person. I also wanted to make a worldwide impact by inspiring others to follow their dreams.

I felt like I could keep surfing big waves forever, but what would be the *ultimate* challenge? What could I do that could inspire other people on such a massive level?

That's when Micky said to me, "Well, what is something that's impossible?"

I nearly spit it out: "That bloody Night Rider project!"

It was a challenge. It was something that had never been done before. It was something that seemed impossible. And in some ways, it seemed inevitable, like fate was showing up again, because I hadn't really been able to let it go.

Random people would see me at parties and ask, "Wouldn't it be cool if you could surf a big wave at night?"

I would look at them in shock, wondering if they knew I'd actually tried it once. But no one knew, because I kept this one in the vault. I hadn't told a soul. It would trigger that little thought again, but I would soon forget about it. Then six months later something like that would happen again. It was just enough to keep it lingering. It wasn't until I had that heartfelt chat with Michael Maidens that I realized that I needed to see if Night Rider was possible.

Until that moment, I wanted to be one of the best big-wave surfers in the world, but for my ego, so I could prove I was good enough.

There's totally nothing wrong with that, but it wasn't me. That wasn't my true purpose. When you're doing something that's not aligned with your true purpose and passion, you don't have endless energy. You know that's not the calling of your core, and you feel flat about it.

When I was truthful with myself, I realized that I was still trying to prove to myself that someone (me) who had nothing, who came from nothing, who didn't have an upbringing from somewhere with big waves, could be any good.

During that awesome talk with Micky, I realized that if I actually ever did go on to be any good at big waves, I would be the best true example of someone who came from nothing to achieve this. Being one of the best big-wave surfers was no longer about me; it was now about setting an example to inspire people to go after their dreams.

Because in the grand scheme of things, even though I had a three-year contract to chase all the big swells, I was still at the bottom of the pecking order because I was so new and hadn't done my time yet. Even though I did have the opportunity to travel the world, I didn't have a massive salary. The surfers who had a lot of credibility were paid a great salary and could live like rock stars. The big brands that sponsored them were running multiple magazine advertisements, and that gave them a lot of credibility and put them on a pedestal. The brands also ran the big-wave events, and it was hard to get into them unless you were sponsored by their company or were one of the bigger fish who'd been around a while and were really well known.

So here was the thing: if someone who had zero credibility in this space who wasn't a big name and didn't have a huge backing could go and night-surf a big wave, then anyone could do anything. It would set a 100-percent true example that if I could do it, then so could anyone else. Maybe that would encourage others to take the risks, take the steps, and go after their own Big Wave.

But I also needed the proof myself. I'd been doing all this training and following the steps Steve had taught me. I wanted to see if it was real—if a normal person could do extraordinary things. Could I turn my dream into a reality? Or was I delusional?

TAKING THE FIRST STEPS FORWARD

A lot of people have surfed small, perfect point breaks and fun waves in the late evening or at night, and have done so for years. But no one had ever attempted to surf a big wave at night. With no light source, it would be suicide. I'd done those few trial runs with the headlamp where the cord nearly choked me, but if there was another light source—it might really be possible.

I needed to take personal responsibility for my vision: I could somehow make this work if I made it my priority. After all, I'd taken that same approach many times before, and that persistence and hard work paid off.

I wanted to run this crazy idea by Steve White. He'd always been so generous with advice, and I knew he'd give me his honest opinion. I visited him in his office at Burleigh. Up until this point he had always been encouraging me to follow my dream and do the things I wanted to do, to believe in myself, and that anything is possible. The first thing he said when I told him about the Night Rider project was, "You're going to do *what*?"

As we sat and talked and I told him how I was going to go about planning this, he started to get excited and even got goose bumps. He gave me nothing but encouragement from then on and was always patient as he listened to me talk about the next steps.

As the project progressed, he also checked my strategy, and he was pleased that it always seemed like I was ahead of the curve. I felt like I was in a scene in *Karate Kid* when Mr. Miyagi gives Daniel his approval. I had a pattern of taking risks since childhood, but my determination had always paid off. Now I was finally coming to an understanding of what life was all about, and how I would be setting an example for others if I succeeded.

When I'd asked for a surfboard for my 11th birthday, and my mum said, "Are you sure you don't just want a better bodyboard?" I'd stepped up, taken a chance, and asked for what I really wanted. When I got dead last in the Nippers paddling contest when I was just a kid, I still knew I could be good if I practiced. And when I'd made up my mind that I was going to stop surfing small waves, the results had been better than I could have ever imagined.

I had the determination. Now I just needed a plan, but not just a list of things to do or people to call. I did something Scott suggested—I created a business plan. At first I thought it was the stupidest thing ever. I thought, *Well, I'm a surfer; I don't need to write a business plan.*

He said, "Just fill it out; it will help you understand how you are going to do all the things that you are going to do." When I protested again, he said, "Your dream isn't going to happen unless you have a clear outline of what that actually is." According to Scott, this was the part that actually made everything clear, and this was the part that set everything up. I could at least see the value in that, so I agreed to do it.

Following a template he sent me, I put some serious effort into it and identified what could go wrong and how to prepare for it. I knew what it would take, at least initially, and what obstacles would need to be overcome.

I remember thinking, *This has no relevance to what I am doing*, but actually it really did. It was about getting clear on what I had, what I could contribute as an athlete right then, what I thought I needed, and all the things I thought I would have to overcome to be able to achieve my goal.

I also needed to assess my risk and set up safety nets of procedures for how we could evacuate someone in the event of something going wrong. It might sound like overkill, but the purpose of doing a risk analysis as part of a business plan is so that once you've listed out every obstacle you can think of, every area where you might need help, when you're actually in the midst of the project, what seems like it should be the most chaotic situation remains pretty calm.

I'd prepare for the worst-case situation and then plan to train for that to gain confidence and truly feel like there was no stone left unturned. But I made sure that I was also always expecting the best-case scenario to happen, so that my thoughts were aligned with my goals.

Because I'm a visual learner, I drew pictures of how I thought each piece of equipment would look and where it would be placed—a blueprint sketch of an invention, so to speak. Then I drew pictures to try to explain what I wanted to do, because no one really understood, and the images clarified my thoughts as I was explaining them to others. I drew a guy on a surfboard with a special vest and put all the lights where I thought the lights needed to be. I had a light on the back of the surfboard and all these little inventions that I thought I would need—like a built-in solar panel to charge the lights in the surfboard, built-in foot straps, and a switch for the lights that would be on my vest. I drew about 10 different pictures in total. A friend who was a cartoonist drew them a bit more detailed for me to show someone else if I ever had the opportunity.

I stayed up night after night getting this business plan done. I made this rule with myself that I wasn't going to go off and chase another big wave until I had written out the plan, thinking it was like a 30-minute kind of booklet and I could just fill it in and off I'd go. Instead it took four nights in a row until probably 4:00 in the morning, trying to get really specific and detailed about every single piece of it.

That was the clearest plan I'd ever had—and certainly ever written. Now I knew what I wanted the finished version of my plan to look like. It was a blueprint, the internal secret coding of how this whole masterpiece was going to be played out.

I had no clue that just two weeks later, I'd actually have the opportunity to present it to a potential investor. Nor did I even have a clue that I'd need an investor until I wrote out the bloody business plan.

A MAN WITH A PLAN

I didn't have the money to do any advertising, and I didn't know how to attract investors or outside help. But I'd had a vision that someone who understood the business world would come out of nowhere. I never imagined that link would come through my next-door neighbor.

Often when I was outside cooking on a barbecue, I'd look up and see my neighbors in their yard, and I'd wave. That was how I'd met my neighbor, by being kind and introducing myself. That, and the fact that right after they moved in, their dog broke into our backyard and smashed up all our potted plants trying to dig into the new potting mix we'd just put in. I ended up wrapping a rope around his dog collar, taking him over to his house, and introducing myself.

Now I'd known this guy for years and obviously knew that he was really successful at what he did, but I didn't know what that was. I had never really asked, and the question never came up until I was aware that I might need help from someone who had a lot of business acumen.

Once it was clear from my business plan that I needed a team to help, I felt like I was tuning in to a radio frequency that I had never listened to ever before. As soon as I tuned in, I could hear it and see it everywhere.

My neighbor was having a birthday party, and I'd agreed to come over. I'd actually hurt myself surfing, but I had this rule, thanks to the work I'd done years before with Steve White, that I would be a man of my word. So even though I regretted telling my neighbor I would go, I hobbled over anyway, an ice pack strapped to my ankle.

There was a guy at the party who was pretty drunk. The Ferrari in the driveway belonged to him. It turned out he was my neighbor's best friend. Even though I wasn't right next to him, I could hear him chatting about how he had just sold one of his businesses and it had done really well. After grabbing a drink, I hobbled past the Ferrari and sat at a nearby table, where the guy that was talking about his business deals started to give me shit. "Oh, look at this wuss sitting in the chair. What did you do, bump your toes or something?" I thought, *Who is this wanker who is giving me a hard time?*

But at some point during the night, after a brief conversation, this guy said, "If you ever need a hand with anything, I would be more than happy to help you."

It wasn't a big party, so there was only a small group of people, and everyone was hanging out within earshot of each other. I thought he was just drunk and talking shit, so I said, "No worries. Thanks, man. I appreciate it." By now I had been at the party long enough, had been able to catch up with my mate, and was ready to go home. But over the next 30 minutes, this guy offered to help me two more times.

The first two times, I wasn't paying attention, but the third time, he was more specific. "If you ever need a hand in the business world, I would be more than happy to look over some things for you."

I thought, *That's the third time this guy has told me that. Wake up! There is something smacking you in the face right now, and you are oblivious.*

This time I said, "Okay, I do actually have something I'm working on, and it's a really, really cool project. I've got a business plan on exactly how it would work and exactly what I would want to do, and if you would have a look at it, maybe I'll see you next week sometime if you're free." I thought by then he would be sober, and if he wasn't full of shit, he'd actually look at it.

We met the next week. When I went into his office, I learned that he wasn't a drunk. He'd been paying attention to what I was saying the whole time. It turns out he's a great guy. He built a hospital, paid for it all, gave it all to charity, and didn't tell anyone! He was just a smart-ass who enjoyed playing tricks and jokes after a few drinks.

He had just sold one of his companies for $90 million and I thought, *What are the chances of me connecting to that by just being a man of my word, honoring what I said I would do?* I fully believe that when you stick to your guns and be who you say you're going to be, opportunities present themselves.

I showed him the business plan that I had spent hours and hours writing, and he and his people looked at it. They could see that there was an opportunity there for themselves, as businesspeople. They said, "We would actually really love to be a part of this. We'd like to get behind it, and you're going to need a lot of help in x, y, and z, because those are areas that you clearly don't know. We will help you, and we will let you be the best you can be in your space."

They provided a full-on team and a thorough explanation of what was ahead, letting me know they had so-and-so who handled the books, so-and-so who did this, another person who would help out with this, and this person who would help me out with that.

I was given access to everything I had written in my business plan—the exercise that I thought was the dumbest thing in the world. And now I had my dream and my vision and my set of skills. I had to bring in people who had other sets of skills and let them shine in their space. It really became a team effort, as it was no longer me trying to take on the whole world to achieve this one goal.

I left that meeting with a full team on board who would help me in every area I could have imagined and more, and we had a budget of more than $1 million to put toward the project.

I also believe that if my vision had been purely based on ego, I wouldn't have had that opportunity. What I wanted to do was really pure, and I believe the opportunity came because my heart and mind were in the right place.

Once I had investors on board—and a whole team on it—the whole thing happened in just six months. We were able to utilize multiple people's talents and skill sets. It was a huge relief to know I didn't have to do it all on my own.

And the guy with the Ferrari—he came off as a rough Aussie, like a Crocodile Dundee kind of guy—but as soon as he was on board, he turned out to be one of the most generous and kind people you could ever meet, always looking out for the family, trying to help in any way possible.

ROOFTOP REALIZATIONS

My team had been trying out one lighting option after another, but everything was failing the night testing. The pressure of the water kept smashing the lights. Some lighting setups cost $4,000, so breaking one each night was frustrating.

Each time left me wondering if it would work if we made a slight change. But after a while, I wondered if we'd ever find the solution.

I'd come home from the night testing around midnight, still dripping wet and sometimes in my wetsuit. I'd put the Jet Skis away, and while everyone else was asleep, I'd climb onto my roof and sit up there alone. It was the only place I could hide while looking at the stars.

Usually the time on my roof would start out the same. I'd reflect on the Night Rider project and wonder, *Is this just the biggest waste of time?* Even though I had the right purpose in mind, having each option still fail was hard. I was so determined and had seen it work in my own head, but then the reality of what I was doing wasn't matching up. That was the part that was really pissing me off. I just didn't know how to make this new technology 100 percent right.

Usually after 30 minutes of being frustrated, I would get to the point where I would be sitting on the roof going, "Right-o, maybe there is no way to move forward." Then I would say to myself, "Is there no other option now?"

Between the team, the experts, and everyone I had spoken to, we had covered every situation that we thought we could, and it all still failed. The lighting technology broke numerous times because the wiring systems couldn't handle the force of impact. The equipment was too heavy to wear and still be safe. The brackets rattled too much, which caused vibrations and set off all the fuses. But there was always that one thought in the back of my head: *Well, maybe there is another way that could have worked.*

It would have been a lot easier to say, "We're up shit creek, so let's just let it go." But I didn't let it go. I couldn't. There was a bigger purpose that was driving me to do this project. I realized that once I achieved this, it would set me free of the doubts and questions about whether or not I could do this.

Of course I doubted myself and the entire project. I thought, "This is all shit. This is not happening. I'm a freaking nutcase." Most nights spent sitting on the roof, I'd feel sorry for myself for a good 10 minutes. Then there was a part of me that went, "Right-o, so we're all done and dusted." But every time, there was another thought that was yelling, "Is it really over?" There was something inside going, "There's another way." Until there was another way, I was just going to keep going.

It would have been self-sabotage to say, "Let me get out of not fulfilling what could be something special," because when you really look at it, if you need it, it's there. People come out of the woodwork. The investors came on board for Night Rider, and it was just bizarre.

Every night on the roof, my thoughts tumbled around in my head, each of them competing for the win. But eventually there would be silence. And every time, just as I was about to climb down, some other way, some other idea or option would pop into my head and I'd perk up, thinking, *Ah, shit! I haven't tried this yet!*

It was like I was having my own little self-psychology sessions up on the roof. Each time I went up frustrated. And each time I came down with some excitement that there was still another way. It would make me feel like Lloyd in the movie *Dumb and Dumber* when he asks Mary what the chances are that they could be together. She says,

"Not good . . . like one out of a million," and he gets all excited even though that's terrible odds.

"So you're saying there's a chance?" Lloyd says with renewed optimism. That's how I felt—still clinging to the tiny chance it would all work out.

GET DEAD SERIOUS

Even after eight different contraptions, the lighting technology would fail. In the very beginning, it had started off being a forward-facing light, which was the one Cryskai's dad suggested. That was dangerous, and I wrote it off. We never went back to that technology.

Then the next thought was, "Okay, what if we had a light attached to the board?" First, we tried duct-taping a giant flashlight to the back of the board and seeing how that worked. It didn't. Then we started with basic submarine lights. They were small but powerful long-beam lights. The submarine lights kept getting caught in all the spray, so maybe it needed to trail behind the board.

Then we had this cord that would let the light drag about five to six feet behind the board, and I had this theory it would bend underwater with the way that the board moved. But I was wrong.

Then we put foils on the light that was five meters behind the board, like a diving fishing lure, so it would swim down low and wouldn't skip out of the water. But once you got to a certain speed, it was impossible to keep that under.

So then we went to light brackets that were literally fiberglassed high onto the board, and facing above where the spray would go. The brackets were at the back of the board, but the impact of bouncing through the waves would just shatter the lights.

The final epiphany was that the light needed to be taken off the board and put up high. That's when we realized if it was on my back, my legs would be like shock absorbers, and it would stop the impact of the lights getting bounced around.

We tried that, and the first trial actually worked! But then the lights failed. We were thrilled about the basic concept, but we needed to figure out what type of lights to use. We got lights that could withstand the bouncing, but they were too heavy. It was like having a brick strapped to my back. I was convinced this light would have sledgehammered a hole in me on a 60-foot wave.

The next step was to refine the light to almost the width and thickness of a ruler. Doug Gavin, the lighting engineer for our project, made it happen. He is a very logical thinker with the ability to see things from a different point of view. He knew a lot about reflection and how light would move and bounce off other objects. The light he created was designed to illuminate a 50-foot building, top to bottom, without being so big that it could kill me. The lights were tiny, but the battery pack was the size and weight of a brick.

It was time to test it. Out in the real event, I would be moving around a lot, and we wanted to see if it would be too heavy. We did an impact test, where I had to sit on a Jet Ski, go up to 80 kilometers an hour, and purposefully fall off on my back. Could the lights handle it? Could *I* handle it?

I climbed out of the water and told the team, "Okay, that is going to beat the shit out of me."

So we had to refine the battery pack to make it lighter, smaller, and thinner, but still have enough power. In the end, we ran three individual light vests that all had thinner battery packs. We knew each vest had five minutes of light, but each wave I was going to ride would go for about 20 seconds max. So, once one light vest would run out of juice, the plan was that I would take off the whole vest and put on a new one. I could have one that would last for 10 minutes, but it was too heavy and dangerous to have that much volume on me in the water. I had no clue how many waves I'd be able to ride, but I wanted to be safe even if I was only able to catch one or two.

We decided to stick with the three separate vests. The surfboards also had red lights inserted into the fiberglass, and the only way to recharge those batteries was to attach them to a solar-powered light panel. We ran with three individual boards, so we'd have a backup in case one got lost or damaged.

My friend Micky was great because he was external to the team, so when we'd catch up, he'd be able to come in with fresh eyes and challenge me to see if everything was rock-solid. He's one of my best friends, but frankly, even though he was helpful, in those days I thought he was a giant pain in the ass. He'd find something we might have overlooked, and I'd be exhausted, having been up all night working on another problem, and now I'd be up all night again working on *this* one. But it would always be to our advantage and forced us to be extra-thorough. And that was what made me so confident in the end—knowing that we'd covered absolutely everything. He was also great about helping me discuss fears and dangers throughout the whole process.

We pushed and pushed until we'd worked on every obstacle. The project as a whole felt terrifying, but we broke it down piece by piece into a series of calculated risks. Now we had the right lights, the right vests, the right surfboards, and a team that believed in the project 100 percent. We were finally getting somewhere.

EXERCISE: CREATE
YOUR BIG WAVE WORKSHEET

No matter what kind of dream you have—whether it requires financial backing, athletic training, or a large investment of time—a great plan can help you get crystal clear on your goals, as well as all the steps you'll need to take along the way to be successful. And since this also requires taking action, we're going to create a cross between a business plan and an action plan with this Big Wave Worksheet.

You have to get a clear picture in your head of the resources needed, the time needed, and the actions needed. Get dead serious about your Big Wave. And create visual references that will help you stay on task.

BIG WAVE WORKSHEET

1. Start with your overall vision. List your Big Wave, or your ultimate goal/dream:

    _____

    _____

    _____

2. Write a brief summary of your goal, including *why* you want to achieve this Big Wave, *who* will be impacted because of it, and *where* it will take place (try to make this fewer than 150 words):

    _____

    _____

    _____

3. Create a deadline for your goal. This can be revised as you go along, but for now we need a measurable date in which you wish to reach your goal:

    _____

4. Create an affirmation to keep you motivated:

    _____

    _____

    _____

    Make at least five copies of this affirmation to place around you in areas you'll see each day. List those five areas here:

    _____

    _____

    _____

    _____

    _____

5. Make a list of possible challenges or restrictions you'll have to overcome. (Does your Big Wave require moving to a new location? Does it require a strict diet or exercise regimen?)

    _____

    _____

    _____

How will you overcome each of these challenges? Plan your strategy for each.

_____

_____

_____

6. Does your Big Wave require financing? If so, how much will you need?

_____

How will you fund your Big Wave (investors, family, friends, savings account, fund-raisers, and so on)?

_____

_____

_____

7. Does your Big Wave require you to purchase/use specific equipment? If so, make a list of what you'll need to buy to achieve your dream.

_____

_____

_____

Can you borrow any of these items from others or purchase them used?

8. Who will be on your team? Even if you have a solo mission, such as running a marathon, you still need a team of people who will support you, encourage you, and hold you accountable.

   _____

   _____

   _____

9. If your Big Wave has multiple parts, who will be responsible for each area?

   _____

   _____

   _____

   Is there a date associated with each task or part?

   _____

10. Create the timeline. First, chart your goal over the time between when you will begin and the deadline you set in #3. If it will take you a year, make a list of the major actions you'll need to complete every month.

    _____

    _____

    _____

    _____

Let's break each month into four weeks. What weekly actions will you need to complete to stay on target for your deadline?

_____

_____

_____

_____

11. Let's say you've reached your goal. Great! How will you celebrate your goal or achievement? List a few ways you can celebrate yourself for a job well done.

_____

_____

_____

_____

Don't forget your team! List what you will do to show appreciation to everyone on your team for their part in your Big Wave.

_____

_____

_____

_____

CHAPTER 5

Step #3: The Power of Pure Intentions

You are imperfect, you are wired for struggle, but you are worthy of love and belonging.

— BRENÉ BROWN

As we talked about a bit in Chapter 4, there's a difference—a big difference—between having pure intentions and doing things for egotistic reasons. You need to understand what your motivation is before the project gets off the ground, because if you're in the game for the wrong reasons, you're likely to fail. I know about this first-hand because it happened to me, when I was only focused on "being the best" as a big-wave surfer. I wasn't thinking about the bigger picture—that I could use my talent to help other people in some way. Instead, I was more focused on the money and the success.

The dissatisfaction I felt during that time was my gut telling me something needed to change.

RECOGNIZING THE WRONG INTENTIONS

Having success in sports often means you'll be asked to be a sponsored athlete or ambassador for a product, or sometimes even be in commercials. That can be a great experience if it's a product you believe in and it strengthens your brand. But it can be a real struggle if it's not truly a product that aligns with your core values and the way you want to represent your brand.

I was asked if I would consider doing a commercial for an alcohol company—not one that produced beer or wine, but the kind of alcohol you drink down in shots at parties. When they approached my manager with the proposal, they wanted me to be perceived as one of the hardest people around. In one brainstorming session for the commercials, someone proposed the idea that I was some ridiculous party guy in a room and there was another group of cowboy people, and we were all in a room drinking shots together, and that's what made these people who they were. Basically, the company wanted to portray that all my success and my personality were fueled by alcohol.

It didn't take even a second for me to realize that was a terrible idea. Not only was it false in my personal life but it was also misleading to the consumer. The fact is I'm a massive lightweight and I drink only three or four times a year. After three drinks I'm in all sorts of trouble—far from the hard-ass person that they wanted me to pretend to be.

When I was 16, I was going on camping trips with my mates and got into drinking and seeing what that was all about. When I was 17 I was going to nightclubs, and I could go into a pub and get served a beer without getting asked for an ID. Sometimes I was able to get into the back doors of nightclubs. I got a real buzz from getting away with all that, and I thought that made me really cool. But by the time I turned 18, the legal drinking age in Australia, I was over it. It wasn't a big deal because I'd already done it and I didn't really drink at all anymore.

So when the idea was originally presented to me, my first thought was, *No way!* I wasn't necessarily against an alcohol campaign, especially if it had been for a red wine or the type of spirits that someone might drink in celebration, because that's who I am. I might drink a good cognac or a small glass of something smooth, and I'll always ask the bartenders to mix it with cola. I've had bartenders roll their eyes at me like, "How could you ruin such a good drink?" Some have even refused to mix it for me, saying that I'd have to mix it in myself. But I don't care—that's what I like, and I'm paying for it! The reality is that if I had four shots of this particular drink, I'd be under the table, unable to walk. That's how badly alcohol affects me, especially when I'm training.

The guys on my management team, as well as my investors, were looking at the numbers and saying, "This is a pretty good thing!" I remember thinking that it went against everything we were doing. But I also remember going back on my initial reaction, thinking maybe I should accept it for financial reasons, since going ahead with this would have made it a lot easier to fund Night Rider. It would also help out the guys on my team, and maybe I should be doing what I can to help them out since they've made such an investment in me. I really wanted to do everything I could to help the people who had helped me. But at what cost?

I remember feeling vulnerable, like, *Shit, do we actually have to discuss this? Or is this something they would consider, knowing that I don't even drink that type of shit?* To me it felt purely like selling out. And I felt stuck. It didn't feel right in the least—even though the money was great. But I knew that it wouldn't set me up for success and it wouldn't set the Night Rider project up for ultimate success, because it wouldn't have aligned with everything we said we wanted to do.

Luckily, my business partners weren't as worried about the financial side as I was. I wanted to help them and give back to them, but they said, "Well, if you don't want to do it, you definitely don't have to do it." I was so happy to be working with guys who weren't going to make me do something just to make money.

THE DANGERS OF HIDDEN AGENDAS

I bet you've had a similar opportunity once or twice in your life, where you were offered some seemingly great opportunity but deep in your gut you knew it wasn't worth it—and not because of the money or the success it might bring—but because you knew somewhere down the line something would be required of you that would have gone against your core beliefs, your morals, or your common sense.

Maybe you are offered a new job or a promotion in your current career, and the financial benefits will be great! But to do your new job, you'll have to make compromises in your personal life that make your gut churn.

Maybe you've recently begun a new relationship, and while it started off with a bang, there have been flashes of abusive behavior that left you confused and wondering if somehow it was your fault that your partner lost their temper. You swore you'd never let anyone mistreat you in a relationship, but you're also tired of being alone, so you're caught in a compromise.

These are not easy situations. They may require deep soul-searching. And while you won't always know the right answer immediately, I guarantee you can tell when you're being tested. There's unease in your mind and body. Something just doesn't feel right. And when something doesn't feel right, you need to take action to resolve the situation. You need to set the right intentions for yourself.

An opportunity coming to you that way can be tempting. And it can initially look like it will solve all your problems. But make sure there are no hidden agendas, no reasons for doing it that aren't right for you and who you want to be.

If my reasons were, "I want to make a lot of money," I would definitely have gone ahead with the alcohol campaign. Or if I wanted to be seen as way cooler than I am, if I wanted to have the kind of image the campaign wanted to project, then I probably would have done it. But that's not why I have sponsors.

If you get an opportunity that seems amazing, make sure it aligns with your heart and your mission because it's much easier to walk away from an opportunity at the beginning than to be stuck in the middle, unable to get out.

SETTING THE RIGHT INTENTIONS

If you have a clear vision, and it is something your heart wants to do, it is a pure intention. But if all of a sudden you are finding that you are burning friendships and going against things that you stand for just to make money, or so that you will become more important than someone else, you are going against those original intentions. You are going against the flow, and you are going against what is right. When you get to that point, you will be dissatisfied because it feels empty. All the meaning and reason you wanted to achieve is lost if you don't have that pure intention.

Are there different types of right intentions? Yes, of course. I think it just comes down to checking in with yourself. Asking yourself, *Am I on my moral compass? Is this in line with my greater vision?* In my experience, every time your actions and your desires are in line with your heart, things like money, ideas, and help flow quickly to you. You will have unlimited energy, and opportunities will just come out of the woodwork.

On the other hand, when you are going against your heart, everything shuts down and there are roadblocks everywhere. There is red tape on everything. You will finally realize, "Oh, I am trying to move forward in the wrong area. I am pushing shit uphill!"

It is much more efficient to have a quick analysis of what's going on and realize that you are off-track. When you get back on the right track, everything starts to flow again. It's not because you are making it happen fast. It's just that everything is happening the way it is supposed to happen.

I've never been happier to miss out on money than when I let go of the alcohol campaign. I felt so lucky to have dodged that bullet—and here's the thing. I believe that if I had only been in search of money, and if I had not put out the intention that I didn't want to do it, somehow the negotiations would have moved forward, despite what I wanted. That could have been disastrous for the Night Rider project, since the pure intention was to inspire people from all walks of life. If I'd done that deal, that intention would have been lost, and the message would have been focused on a product. I realized in that meeting that making money couldn't be one of my driving forces. I didn't want the message to be lost. I wanted to be the best true example of someone who came from zero to achievement, from having a dream and turning it into reality.

My vision was to inspire people of all ages. I would use the platform of achieving the night ride to get people's attention, delivering the message on what was done and how I did it, so that they would understand what they too might be capable of. In order to do that, we had to position ourselves to appeal to everyone, not just other surfers. That was why my title was changed from "big-wave surfer" to "big-wave surfer and ocean adventurer." That was why I couldn't let a brand own my image. My vision would have been lost, and Night Rider would have been about some new board shorts or something.

Mind you, I wasn't being entirely altruistic. This project was also for me to prove to myself that I could achieve what I'd set out to do. I would be seen as successfully doing a world first with high visual impact. It would show my determination to be seen as a leader in the adventure world.

My investors had good reasons for wanting to align with suggested sponsors. It would limit their risk in case it all went south, and I totally supported that. But we agreed that the only sponsors that we would ask were companies that had products that I would actually use in the project, like Jet Skis, or something that suited our image. This meant we still had control over our message.

And then we were approached with the idea of doing a documentary on Night Rider. For all of the above reasons, I was hesitant at first, even though I knew a documentary made a lot of sense. Even so, the production side of it would be such a pain in the ass, because I was discovering things for the first time myself, and I didn't want to deal with shit like being followed around all the time. I wanted to figure everything out for myself, and then I'd be happy to tell them how I did it once I was done—but that's not how documentaries work.

Then one of my coaches said to me, "If you do this project and pull it off—imagine you ride this wave at night, and you actually do it and survive and come back—you are going to inspire us, all of the coaches, all of your family. Everyone on this team will be pumped, and it's really going to be amazing if you do it."

I had to agree with him.

Then he said, "The thing is, it would be really selfish of you if you let only *us* know about it. If you do this for the documentary, you are going to let millions and millions of people see the same story. So stop being such a selfish prick and understand it from this point of view." (And they were right. In the *first week alone* a 30-second highlight aired as a teaser for the documentary, and it got 100 million impressions in America.)

Finally I said, "All right!" I knew there was a bigger cause than just me, and it wasn't such a big sacrifice on my part. I agreed to do the documentary for Night Rider.

The truth is, we took a hit financially. We would have made a lot more money with a big sponsor, and I could have still gotten to live out my own personal mission of surfing Night Rider.

But would the right message have been shared with millions of people—that you can overcome any obstacle with planning, determination, and heart?

Not at all.

The thought of just being cool and badass, or doing it for a brand and making lots of money, felt really empty.

So we went forward on our own terms.

YOU'VE GOT TO BE SOLID ON EVERY LEVEL

Being solid in all areas of your life really does make a difference. Imagine a wheel made out of chain links. Let's say in one area of your life, you are very honest and doing everything in a certain way, but then in another area of your life (your family or your partner), you are treating things differently, maybe being a little less honest. At some point there is going to be so much tension on one of those links that it breaks, and things aren't going to flow easily anymore.

It's a simple way of looking at life, but it's true. A guy who is a very powerful C.E.O. might not think he has time to eat well or exercise, so he eats fast food and drinks high-sugar drinks for energy all day. He works his ass off and makes hundreds of millions, and then he finds out he has cancer. Chances are his lifestyle may have had something to do with it. Now he has to take time off work for treatment, and he has to overhaul his eating habits and exercise. His life is clutching at straws, and there's no limit to the amount of money he'd pay to get it back in order.

I know guys who are so obsessed about fitness that it prevents them from having a healthy relationship. The key is that you have to put in the same kind of positive and intentional energy across *multiple paths*. If there is an area that is lacking, when it breaks down—and it will—it will bring down everything else with it.

We see this happen far too often with professional athletes. A team might have a star player who has incredible speed and amazing strength. But he also has a terrible temper and he's arrested a few times and loses a high-dollar contract (or two). Pretty soon his teammates begin to see his shitty attitude as a distraction and there's dissention in the locker room. You can see how a guy like this can bring the whole team down because they're so reliant on him in one area, but as a team they're not working. The guy is talented, for sure, but his unbalanced life makes him more of a nuisance than a benefit to the team.

Many of my mentors have talked to me about how important it is to be solid in all areas of life. "Before you become a good athlete, you have to become a good person first." It's so true, and I'd extend that not only to athletes but to all careers and goals. You can't expect to be successful for long as an amazing athlete, or a high-powered lawyer, or an entrepreneur who is really making a difference if you are an asshole to everyone you come in contact with.

Of course, there are people who are assholes who appear to be successful, and it's frustrating when we see it, but know that something will always catch up with them down the track. We might see the "onstage performance," the version that they want everyone to see, but backstage their lives might be falling apart.

Do yourself a favor and review the areas of your life right now. If you are lacking in any area—be it fitness or relationships or work ethic or health—think about what you can do today to take one step in the right direction.

IF YOU WANT GREAT RESULTS, DO THE WORK

I firmly believe that what you reap in one area of your life, you'll sow everywhere. You have to have good intentions if you expect to accomplish good things and receive good things.

If you have a problem area, it will drain the energy out of other areas in your life. And if you take shortcuts, you can expect trouble. Of course, I had to learn that one the hard way, just like everyone else.

From the very beginning of this project, I had different people helping out with their areas of expertise: Scott with the business-plan advice, Steve White as a mentor, the investors coming on board, and the lighting engineer . . . everyone came along and presented a part of the project, based on what they knew to do, and then they left, so to speak. They'd give me all they could give me, but the rest was up to me to take it to the next step. Of course, they were there if I needed them, but no one was going to hold my hand. It was my project, and it was up to me to get it done.

If at any point I decided I didn't want to do it, or if I was waiting for someone else to do it for me, the whole project would have been dropped on its head. It's the same with your dream. People will come out of the woodwork to help you, but nothing will happen unless you're willing to put in the effort yourself and step up to every challenge.

During the earlier stages of the Night Rider project, we were so disciplined in the planning side, making sure everything we were doing for Night Rider did not involve any shortcuts. I was really driven and working so hard on breaking down every obstacle. I was checking all the boxes in the paperwork areas, making sure this project was 100 percent safe and doable. Then on the side, I was training three days a week in order to handle the surfing side of things, to make sure that I was in peak physical shape, ready for any big swell that came—otherwise, what was the point of any of this?

Except that I started slacking off in that area because I had so much other shit going on. When I was working with so many different people, my priority changed from just going to every swell and surfing, to taking care of all the other responsibilities.

I started to allow the thoughts that said I was too busy to control my actions. *I'm really busy right now, so I'll just skip the warm-up in training. I don't have time for it because I'm running late.* I would train, but instead of finishing the entire workout, I would stop several minutes short or skip the warm-up entirely because I had to be back to the office to do some things. The truth is that I didn't *have* to be back in the office. The office would still be there when I was done training. But I made the office work a bigger priority than my training, and it came back to bite me in the ass.

When I was focused on office work, I lost focus on taking responsibility for myself. If I was truly taking responsibility for myself, like Steve White said, I would have made myself get up a little bit earlier, or finish whatever I was doing beforehand a little earlier so I would have time for everything I needed to do in my training. I wasn't overloaded. I just needed to allow for more time and take full responsibility. I took the shortcuts instead—no one forced me to do that.

I did this six weeks in a row, cutting training short, missing warm-ups, not doing the cooldowns—skipping or half-assing the basic things I always do that keep me in great condition. I told myself that I skipped on those because I was trying to get other stuff done.

Then a few months later on a random training session, I drove a Jet Ski through a wave to pick someone up and was knocked unconscious when I went through the wave. I snapped my ankle in three places and had a complete tear in three ligaments. It was one of the worst breaks you can ever have. It was brutal. For a surfer, the ankle is key, and that injury leveled me big-time. I was sidelined for about four months during a crucial time.

The thing is, it was an injury that never should have happened. The fact that I was even putting myself in that situation was a clear indication that my head wasn't in the right place. I was rushing and making choices I wouldn't normally make. When it came time to do this water drill, I hadn't even done the preapproach training that I wanted to do, and I was driving the Jet Ski into serious waves with 40 other things in my head. That was basically like driving in there blind, and, of course, I wiped myself out.

By taking a shortcut to get something else done faster, I tore up my ankle because my muscles were tight. And why did I have tight muscles? Because I had been skipping warm-ups and cooldowns and not doing my entire workout. If your hamstrings are too tight, that leads to your calves being too tight, and so on, until the minute there's an impact, there's so much tension that things snap. Whereas if you're pretty nimble, there's a chance that those kinds of injuries don't actually happen.

The doctor said, "How did this happen? You are doing all this training! This shouldn't have happened!"

I was honest with him, and with myself. "Well, shit, I haven't been doing all the stuff I was supposed to be doing." I knew I had been cutting the training back massively, cutting it short, missing this and that. Or I'd go into a training session totally overwhelmed with everything else.

It's a clear example of too much emphasis in one area—not having an even flow—and then bang, a link in the chain snaps. The result was that suddenly I couldn't surf and couldn't train. I was going to be out for a while, and that was a huge dent in the program. It made me realize that you have to find a way to stay in the flow, because if you try to take any shortcuts, you are going to put too much pressure somewhere else, and eventually something is going to snap. In my case, it was my ankle!

That incident put off the filming for three months and stopped a lot of the things we were doing. Karma kicked me in the ass, and in an instant, I'd gone back three steps because I had tried to jump forward four.

These injuries and the time they cost were unfortunate and detrimental to the entire project. But here's the worst part: When I had the ankle injury, it set me (and everyone else) back three months. When I was skimping on my training three days a week, do you want to guess how much time I actually saved? When I skipped my warm-ups, that would normally save me 15 minutes at the start. The cooldowns might have been a 5- to 10-minute kind of thing. My entire training routine should have normally been one and a half hours max, including the warm-ups and cooldowns, but I was shortening it down to an hour or so. It may not seem like much, but over time, every day, that missed time took its toll on my body.

So let's say that over the course of a week, I cut out three hours of training. For the six weeks I was doing this, that's 18 hours total. *That's not even a day's worth of work*, and it took away three months from me. It was so stupid. I thought I was getting ahead, but instead, back I went.

Would it have mattered if I'd skipped just one day of a full training session? Probably not. There was some leeway. And, yes, sometimes life just happens and unforeseen things come up that you have to deal with. But if you let the half-assed behavior become a pattern, if you divide your attention unevenly, it will eventually slap you in the ass.

So if you have the right intentions for your Big Wave, take the extra time and do the necessary work. Don't skimp or make excuses for why you can't do the work. Because when your one shot comes—you need to be ready to act.

EXERCISE: WHAT ARE YOUR INTENTIONS FOR YOUR BIG WAVE?

We've seen the benefits of your Big Wave Worksheet, but here we're going to dig a little deeper and utilize lists to help get clarity on your intentions and whether they will support your success.

What are my intentions (what do I want to happen) for my Big Wave?

1. _____

2. _____

3. _____

4. _____

What are some positive outcomes that can occur when I accomplish it?

1. _____

2. _____

3. _____

4. _____

Who will these positive outcomes benefit? And why?

1. _____

2. _____

3. _____

4. _____

Are there any negative outcomes that could occur?

1. _____

2. _____

3. _____

4. _____

How will I deal with any negative outcomes?

1. _____

2. _____

3. _____

4. _____

Will accomplishing my Big Wave help me feel successful? Yes ___ No ___

As you check your key goals and the reasons for them, are you also checking to see whether they are in line with your greater vision? Are they aligned and supportive of success? Does the feeling of accomplishing those things fit well with your heart? If they do, you're well on your way to success.

If they don't, take some time to discover which areas don't feel right. And don't ignore them! There's always a reason for hesitation, and you have to figure out how to proceed.

CHAPTER 6

STEP #4: FOCUS ON WHAT YOU DO BEST, DELEGATE THE REST

If you really want to grow as an entrepreneur, you've got to learn to delegate.

— RICHARD BRANSON

In order to accomplish your Big Wave, along with planning and preparation, there's immense value in building a team. A Big Wave is not something you can do by yourself. Of course, at its heart, it's just you and your dream, but an endeavor of this size requires a more varied set of skills than any one person could possess.

Everyone has talents and strengths, and you may be able to take on a great deal of the responsibility for your own Big Wave. But you simply cannot do everything that needs to be done and still be sane.

OPENING UP TO HELP

Remember the night of the barbecue, when the guy who became one of my investors offered to help? The first two times he offered, I ignored him because I assumed he was drunk. On the third time, it was like something in me woke up and I realized that this was what I needed. Even if the guy had turned out to be a fake, I still needed to put myself out there. I'd just gone through the exercise of creating a business plan, and if anything was going to come of it, I'd have to share it with other people eventually.

It wasn't an issue of pride or self-reliance in that moment. I think it was more that I wasn't completely clear on all the steps I'd need to take along the way, so even though I had this initial plan, I wondered if it was good enough to share, or if there were pieces missing. Here's the thing: something like the Big Wave Worksheet is just the first draft of an idea. Of course there will be missing pieces! But you have to start somewhere, and you can't let the fear of not knowing all the answers stop you from sharing your dream with others and stop you from moving forward.

But I paid attention to my intuition. If the same things come around a few times in a row, that's happening for a reason. Something is sending you a message, but you are not hearing it. The first couple of times I was being nudged to listen to this guy and let him help me, I stayed oblivious. But the third time around, I was able to ask myself, *Am I paying attention to everything that's going on? Is there something in this? My head is telling me this guy is a loose cannon and he is half-drunk, but my gut is telling me to pay attention.* So, I went ahead and told him about the project. I had to battle my head to pay attention to my gut—and I'm glad I did!

EXERCISE: ASKING FOR HELP

Knowing what you need help with is important. It's equally important to then take action and actually ask for that help! I had this clear vision of riding the wave at night and what that would look like, but I wasn't clear on how I was actually going to get to that point. I worked my way back and then understood it going forward. Once I was really clear on those steps, I was able to ask for help.

While I don't think you need to prepare a one-minute "elevator speech," or a rehearsed and well-written description of what you're planning to do, I do think you need to be able to convey your goal honestly. Some people might be able to spin something amazing in 90 seconds, but they could be full of shit. Whereas other people might be a little less articulate but as pure as the heart and soul comes. I think the intention is what really matters, and that's what people listen to.

Genuine people are attractive. There is a different energy about them. And they are able to convey that in their explanation. So now you're going to write a brief recap of your Big Wave and your reasons behind it.

- What's your Big Wave?

- Why are you passionate about this goal?

- Who do you want to inspire?

- Who else will be on your team?

- How will you feel once you accomplish this?

- Who can you ask for help? List at least four people who can help you, whether it be with brainstorming, encouragement, accountability, or a more involved role in your Big Wave.

- Now set a date to have a conversation with them. Don't put it off until you have "the perfect plan." You can gain amazing insight that you haven't considered before, once you share your ideas with others.

Now that you've written these answers out, go back and read them out loud. Don't feel silly about it. There is great power in speaking your dreams out loud. Hearing them from your own mouth often makes them more real to you and gives you an additional feeling of excitement and determination to get it done!

IDENTIFYING YOUR STRENGTHS

For several years, I was competing in small waves on the WQS tour and was putting a great deal of energy into that. And when I would compete in a place where the waves were bigger, I would do quite well. It was really obvious that my strengths were in the bigger surf, but it took me a while to finally acknowledge that was what I wanted to do. Had I tried to muscle my way through the frustration in getting better at small surf, I wouldn't have been working to my strengths.

I use football analogies a lot, because I've done a lot of work with conditioning coaches. If there were a football player who was an extremely fast sprinter, but he wasn't as good of a tackler and he wasn't as good at kicking, most people would say, "We've got to really focus on making him a great kicker and an even better tackler." But these conditioning coaches would say, "No, let's focus on making his strengths even stronger. Let's make him even faster, because that is something he is already good at." They would use his strengths to make him far better at that one particular thing, rather than making him all-around "okay." He would be much more of an asset to the team by being superior in one area than mediocre in several. And that's true of all teams, regardless of the type of project.

At the start of the Night Rider project, I thought I needed some big-wave guys with me, but that's when I realized if my team consisted of several guys who all had the same strengths as I did, I was going to have a pretty limited team. You are going to need someone who understands just the pure training elements. You are going to need someone who understands the business elements. You are going to need someone who is excellent at strategizing. I needed a diverse team, and that's what I ended up building.

Some members of the team were just brilliant at seeing obstacles that the rest of us couldn't see, and others were great at managing those obstacles. We brought people from all different areas rather than sticking with a group who all love and do the same thing.

When you're identifying strengths and building a team, I think you have to straightaway ask, "What do you like doing?" Normally the things you like doing are things you are good at doing. If you ask a kid, "Do you want to go for a swim or a run?" the kids who are great swimmers will want to go for a swim, and the kids who are great runners will want to go for a run.

It starts with passion. If you know what you are passionate about, it is normally what you are going to be good at. Obviously you will then get feedback in life, whether you are good at that thing, or maybe you might be suited for something else—just like I figured out I wasn't that great at small-wave surfing. But you can usually figure out pretty quickly what your strengths are and where your interests lie—and they'll usually work together really well.

Being in a team environment when I was a kid really helped me identify my strengths. When I played football, I was always the captain, so I knew I was a good leader, and I was a good "people person." I was great at communicating and inspiring. When it came to schoolwork, I knew I was shit at English and great at math.

Later on in life, I already knew the areas that I was good at and the ones I was pretty average at. That's how I was able to gauge the areas I was good at for the Night Rider project—and which ones I needed to hand off to others.

It really comes down to not having an ego. Let's say you are in a meeting and there's a need for a math specialist. Now you think you are pretty good at math, but there's a dude next to you who is in accounting. You are probably not going to raise your hand and say, "I'll take that role." You already know that other person *specializes* in that area and he is going to have a better understanding. But on the other hand, when you know an area front to back so well, you almost fight for that position because it is something you really feel you can add value to.

I was great at surfing and leadership and overall vision, but there were plenty of things I wasn't good at doing. Some of the guys I've worked with say, "Mark is amazing at coming up with visions of what he wants to do, and then he has to work backward." And they are right. I am good at having a vision of the finished product, the goal, but I'm not so great at considering all the little steps along the way. I would come up with these ideas, and I would think they were so awesome, but I had no idea how to get from here to there. I can say honestly that if I had gone ahead with Night Rider without help, I probably would have died.

Envisioning the steps in between was something I got better at, but at the beginning I couldn't identify the obstacles in the path of the goal as quickly as I could envision how the goal would unfold (like actually riding the wave). I'd overlook what seemed, to me, like little things—like actually learning how to swim in the dark.

I thought, *How hard could it be?* I would sound so confident that everybody would presume that I had already done it. Then when they would ask me, I'd have to admit, "No, I've never trained underwater in the night."

And then they were like, "Yeah, we are going to have to break that down to get it right."

Thankfully I was smart enough to listen to them. I'm so grateful I had those amazing people to pick up the slack in the areas where I wasn't as strong.

ALIGNING WITH THE VISION

When setting up your team, remember that all members need to have the same vision. That's a crucial part. They don't all need the same strengths—it's better if they have different strengths—but they do need to be on board with the ultimate goal.

If just one person had laughed in disbelief or made some facial expression indicating that they didn't think Night Rider was possible, that would have been cancer to the group. Nobody on my team had any doubts that it could be done. Even the person taking notes at the meetings was on board.

That's not to say I didn't welcome discussion. I said, "I need you to understand what I'm doing, and if anyone has any thoughts as to why this wouldn't be the way to do it, please tell me your thoughts." I was encouraging my team to take responsibility for their thoughts and actions and ask questions. It was also me admitting that I didn't have all the answers and being okay with asking, "Have I missed anything? Can you see anywhere that I am wrong?"

If you put your ego aside, you won't be afraid of receiving feedback that says you are wrong or might have missed something. That feedback might possibly save your life or enhance the work project that you are doing. A lot of people don't want to be told they've done something wrong, so they're afraid to allow or ask for feedback. Here's what I think—you have only done something wrong if you are not willing to accept that you could do something better.

TRUSTING THE TEAM

We've talked about building the team and bringing in others who have different skills than you do. We've also talked about utilizing multiple people's talents and skill sets, so let's go to one of the most important points: trust the team and stick with the plan. Do you have a written-down plan of attack? Did you complete the Big Wave Worksheet already? Do you know who will be on your team? Once you've worked out a plan and a team, trust that team and stick with the plan in the face of adversity.

The reason it is so important to have everyone on the same plan is not only so that you don't have any doubt-ers in the group, but also so that when shit hits the fan (because it most likely will at some point), everyone knows how things were intended to go, and everyone can get right back on track. In our planning sessions, we ask the team, "What if this happens? What would we do if that happens?" If things swerve left, everyone in the group knows how to get it straight. You don't want to have any doubters who might say, "I told you this wouldn't work." Any dissonance can cause chaos in the group.

Now even if you prepare perfectly, shit can still go wrong. Your goal isn't necessarily to prevent anything from going wrong—there's only so much you can control, anyway. But the key is to be so prepared that when something does go wrong, you have a backup plan.

Six months before Night Rider actually happened, we did a recon and set everything up to see how it would all work. We went to that level so that when something went askew, we were like, "Right-o, how do we realign? How do we set that up?" It happened like clockwork. We did a SWOT analysis (which stands for strengths, weaknesses, opportunities, and threats). We went through the motions, and we were also very aware of the possible obstacles. If something happened in one area, we'd have a contingency plan for it.

If you've ever worked with elite military groups, they are very big on this type of planning and practice. They are not running by the seat of their pants—there are plans and backup plans for everything. You eliminate fear when you do things that way. There's no chaos, no panicking— it's preparing for the worst and training for the best while visualizing the ideal outcome.

When you've got a team you trust, you can go all in knowing that no matter what happens, you've got their back and they have yours. And you can move forward together.

CHAPTER 7

STEP #5: WORK OUT THE WORST-CASE SCENARIOS

One thing that makes it possible to be an optimist is if you have a contingency plan for when all hell breaks loose.

— RANDY PAUSCH

You might be wondering how I got the courage to do something as potentially life-threatening as Night Rider. I can assure you that I'm not typically a daredevil type of person, so it wasn't because I wanted a huge adrenaline rush or to see if I could cheat death. The real answer is that when it came down to it, my team had mapped out and worked through every danger, fear, obstacle, and scenario so well that it took a majority of the emotional fear out of the picture entirely. I got input from experts, so I understood each and every possible pitfall—as well as the pitfalls of my own fear. I also created a process for reducing the potential difficulties to bite-size pieces.

It was all logistics at that point, and a mix of logistics and training does wonders for stamping out a good bit of the fear associated with such a huge dream. When you are able to get past much of the fear you've been holding on to, there's a beautiful sense of freedom to move forward in your full potential.

FROM FEAR TO FREEDOM

As a kid, I was always afraid of any deep water. In case you're wondering, no, I wasn't afraid of the bathtub. But you'd better believe I avoided the sheep's trough after my near drowning. It wasn't until the first time I got on a surfboard that I realized there was something more powerful than my fear. I had to embrace it and work through it, little by little, if I was ever going to grow.

When you have fear and you are able to break it down into small pieces, and then constantly eliminate the smaller fears, then it can dissolve. For me, in the water I was afraid of drowning. To break that down, even as a little kid, my thought process was this: *Okay, I can wear my floaties in the water. I can learn to swim properly, and I can learn how to tread water.*

Then I thought, *Well, in the ocean I can't control the currents and how the waves move.* So I had to break that down. I had to understand the ocean and tides, understand what rips are, and understand all the smaller things that I was afraid of. What if I was stuck in a rip? What was I going to do? So, not only did I have to be a good swimmer to handle water, I had to be a *really* good swimmer to handle the ocean for when I got stuck in those situations. Then I started preparing for that risk.

I was able to learn all of these things when I was in the junior lifeguard program, Nippers. That's the most beautiful thing about Nippers. They teach kids what a rip is, what it does, and what you do if you are stuck in a rip. You also learn what to do if you are stung by a jellyfish. You learn how to help a friend if they are stung by a jellyfish. You learn survival skills about ocean safety. Once you understand it, you are not fearful, because they've covered all the unknowns. That's why kids' programs like Scouts or junior lifeguarding or martial arts are so great, because they help children understand their surroundings and possible circumstances, and that helps eliminate fear. Fearless kids are able to grow into fearless adults who know how to approach a risk, dismantle it into smaller pieces, and work around obstacles to reach their goals.

It's a fact: if you're going to accomplish anything great, there's going to be some fear. But you can't just ignore it and hope it will go away. Fear is a great teacher; it gives us information about what we need to look at and overcome. If you break each obstacle into smaller pieces, you can see them as they are, take out the negative emotion, and get to work. Because once you know how you're going to address each and every risk, you no longer need to be afraid. You have a plan! And your plan will help you succeed.

GET CLEAR ON THE FEAR

Saying you're going to overcome fear is one thing; doing it takes work! I also don't want to minimize any of the fears associated with your Big Wave. Your fears are totally valid, but you can overcome them with planning and action. And you might as well start at the top with really looking at what you're afraid of—the worst-case scenarios.

As we got closer to Night Rider happening, I was still scared, but I wasn't scared of drowning. I wasn't scared of getting stuck underwater. I wasn't scared about getting attacked by a shark. I wasn't scared about so many things, because I was able to eliminate those fears with training and planning. The only fear was the unknown new experience, and that was okay.

> **CASE STUDY: FLOW (WWW.HONEYFLOW.COM)**
> This Australian-designed beehive raised over $1 million in crowdfunding in less than three hours. Stuart and Cedar Anderson devised a sustainable means to collect honey without disturbing the bees, and the honey is on tap and able to be jarred in minutes.

I knew that any fear would occupy my attention, attention I needed available in order to stay on the wave. Had I not done all the preparation, I might have been shitting myself constantly for 10 waves, or one wave might have been so frightening that I would have a meltdown. I might have just decided I couldn't handle it—and that would have been the end of my dream.

When people learn about all the preparation and training, they might look at Night Rider and think, "That seems like a pretty achievable task." But if they didn't know what went into it, it would be easy to say, "Man, he's a psycho. He's a massive risk-taker." In truth, the risk was extremely calculated, almost to the point where we made it boring and overly safe. (Not really, but you know what I mean.)

The same thing can happen in business. If we hear about someone who just made $30 million on a sale, we can't even imagine all the risks they took to achieve that sale. We can't fathom all those little obstacles they had to overcome. But if we were to understand their plan, we might realize that they were operating in the borderline to safety stretch zone the whole way, meaning it might seem like they were working beyond their capabilities, but in fact, they were actually operating within their comfort zone. They were never in the 100-percent maxed-out zone. Things were always under control, even as they continued to push themselves. That's when you understand you can apply these same principles to anything you want to do.

Here's the thing—fear can make you overdo it, and that's dangerous. When you're hunting for your Big Wave, you never want to be in a constant state of being 100 percent maxed out, because that's a big risk. If you're operating at 100 percent, you don't have time to feel or see the things that could pop up. It will also leave you burned out, and you won't see other opportunities as they come. If you're close to 100 percent, you should start delegating things to the rest of your team so your chain won't snap.

Most successful people operate at 85 percent. They're not cruising along at 60 or 70 percent; they're right up there operating in their strengths. They're using the majority of everything they've got, but there's enough leeway so that if they need to do something else or change direction, they can. It won't break their momentum or cause the whole project to stop. And that's how *you* should operate, as well.

Knowledge is what gives you the power and the confidence. When you understand something, you can break it down into small manageable steps, and you can work at an optimal level. And then the fear is gone.

BREAK EACH FEAR INTO SMALL STEPS

Fear is just a collection of beliefs. When we break each fear into small steps, we can overcome each part with logic and training.

In my case, we wanted to remove the fear of drowning. It wasn't high on my list of fears—I'd gotten over that one long ago—but with Night Rider, drowning became a real possibility, since we couldn't predict everything that might happen. What we could do was guard against it by training and by breaking it down into small pieces.

Let's use the fear of drowning as an example:

Fear: If went under, I wouldn't know which way was up in the dark.

Small step: Learn to recognize or feel which direction the air bubbles are going.

Small step: Learn to feel which way you're floating in the water—up or down.

I was already extremely fit as a big-wave surfer, but I needed to take things to another level. I had been working with a former Special Forces commando, Scott Hipwell, for several years already to help me train for big-wave surfing, but now we needed to take it to another level and push harder than I'd ever gone before. Scott designed a series of intense training drills to prepare me for surviving a repeated pummeling from the brutal force of big waves like Jaws and how to handle it while being totally disoriented at the same time. I needed to be 10 times stronger and more powerful than ever before, and to stay on my board when I couldn't even see where I was going, relying on core strength.

The biggest fear I had was being held underwater, since drowning is the most common killer of surfers, so I needed the lung capacity to hold my breath underwater for long periods of time. I had already trained extensively to hold a four-minute breath, during my years of work as a daytime big-wave rider. Four minutes felt like an eternity. But it could save my life.

To amp it up, my free-diving coach, Anthony Williams, ranked number three in the world, made sure I was comfortable underwater, even more than I already was. He trained most of his clients to hold their breath for three to three and a half minutes. Anthony taught me new relaxation techniques to help me hold my breath for that long, which took a lot of practice. After all the hard-core training, reviewing the location, the height of the waves, and the force they were capable of generating, he thought I needed to be able to hold my breath for closer to five minutes. I was able to work up to 6:04.

When we did my pool training, Anthony blindfolded me, spun me around, and dragged me down to the bottom of the swimming pool so I didn't know which way was up. He taught me that if I blew a bubble and it ran down my face that I was upside down, and I needed to flip myself around and swim upward to the top of the water. When you're holding your breath for a long period of time, it can make you anxious. It's not an enjoyable process. Thankfully, with practice, I was able to find my way to the surface blindfolded.

This isn't all to say that you can magically erase your natural fears through this process. Healthy fears are there to keep you safe—to help you survive. But you can make great progress in chipping away at your fear, cutting it down to a healthy size, if you approach it in a systematic way. You can do that by writing down your fear and then making a list of as many steps as you can think of that will help you gain knowledge in that area, become more comfortable, and eventually remove a great deal of the uncertainty around your fear.

I have always been afraid of sharks, and I was really worried that if I was out in the night paddling a long distance, sharks were just going to be circling behind me and attacking me. I didn't like the idea that I wouldn't be able to see them or tell where they were coming from. But the reality is if they are going to come at you in the middle of the day, they are going to come really fast and you are not going to see where they are coming from then, either.

Also in order to lessen that fear, I did research on how often sharks really circle prey at night. In my research I found that they're hardly ever up on the surface at night. They feed on the bottom of the reefs, so they would be looking for fish that are asleep there. It is highly unlikely that they would ever be circling on the top of the water at night.

That research eased the tension a bit, but I took it a step further by taking action. I did a 16-mile night paddle to overcome my fear of sharks. I drove out to sea in a boat at 9:30 on a Friday night with a few teammates in the pitch black. They dropped me off with my board and said, "Paddle back to shore in the dark."

They were supposed to stay nearby as a support crew boat, and they did, but they still lost me six times. I paddled for about four and a half hours straight to find the beach. All the while, I thought they were tricking me because I could hear them yelling out my name in the dark, and I thought they were just trying to scare me and pretend they had lost me. I'm glad I didn't realize they really had!

In the distance, miles and miles away, I could see tiny little specks, which were high-rises, to focus on where I was headed. For two hours of that four-hour paddle, I was constantly thinking that there was a shark or something near me.

I would paddle and hit a little fish and it would skid in front of me, and I was like, "Oh, fuck."

Then I'd calm down and I'd get back to normal, and then 20 minutes later I'd touch a jellyfish and it would just scare the shit out of me. Every time I hit a jellyfish, I thought it was a shark behind me. It was just a good two and a half hours of constant mental torture of just being paranoid that this was happening.

I'd been paddling for about three hours when my arms began cramping, and I'd been nursing a headache from serious dehydration for the last two hours, but I saw the city lights on land and knew I wasn't too far from home.

It wasn't until I pushed through to the very end that I realized it was the same as during the day. When I put my hand up and I could see shadows inside shadows, I realized my eyes had actually adjusted. I started to understand new things about being in the dark.

My adrenaline was maxed out by the time I walked onto the beach, having cursed up a storm and been scared to death every time I touched something in the water. But I'd done it. By doing that drill, I overcame those massive fears.

And I'm sure I confused the hell out of a guy on the beach.

Since it was a Friday night, there was a guy drunk off his head sitting on the beach, and he saw me come out of the dark with this giant yellow surfboard. He looked at me like I was a ghost. I looked at him and smiled and turned around and went back into the darkness out to the sea. I paddled back out because the boat was back behind the break. The goal was that if I could paddle to the beach, and make it to the shore, then I would overcome that fear. That was the coach's theory, and it was true.

I climbed back onto the boat thinking to myself, *I guarantee you that guy is going to be telling everybody he saw a ghost!*

That was a frightening night, no question. But once I had completed the paddle, all that fear went away. I was scared while doing it, but I never once saw a shark. I realized that being out on the water at night is the same as it is in the daytime. It was really a matter of just seeing the whole thing for what it was and getting over the made-up pictures in my head. That's what we do. We make up a perception of what something is, which often has nothing to do with reality. We create our own problems.

Now it was time for another test.

To overcome my fear of being underwater with sharks, a few days later, the crew took me out to a shipwreck after dark, saying, "It's 100 feet to the bottom, and I want you to free-dive down to the bottom." I knew sharks hung around shipwrecks. You'd think with all the training I'd already done with holding my breath and surviving five hours in the ocean, I'd have nerves of steel by then, but I didn't. I was so scared and over it. I looked down into the water and it looked like black ink. I put my goggles and flippers on, took a few deep breaths, and then, because I was scared, I tried to convince the crew I didn't need to do it. They weren't buying it, so down I went.

Bring trapped underwater in the dark, knowing there's something near you, is a really claustrophobic, eerie feeling. At least I had a guide wire to hold on to, and

Anthony, my free-diving coach, was somewhere nearby in case something went wrong. In the dark, he vanished, so I wasn't sure exactly where he was, and I didn't know how far I was from the bottom since there weren't signs on the rope to indicate my depth, and even if there were, there would have been no light to see them.

When you dive, your chest starts to contract the deeper and deeper you go. Your stomach starts to squeeze in on itself, and the gums at the back of your teeth go numb, so you feel like you're getting squashed. That combined with not knowing everything that's going on around you, you have to tell yourself, "Just keep going. Just keep swimming." You have to calm yourself down. And it's not until you practically run into the bottom that you know you've gone that far down, and you turn around and begin to swim back up.

When I turned around to begin the ascent, I could just barely see the light from the boat at the top of the water, even though it was 100 feet away, and it gave me a sense of relief to know I was getting closer to my next breath.

When I made it back to the top, my body was in shock from lack of oxygen and everything was blurry. My face, ears, and lungs were sore from the pressure, but I remember thinking, *Thank God, I made it.* Even though I was in physical pain, I was grateful I had guys on my team pushing me to my limits and not letting me out of doing it. It gave me so much strength knowing that I had completed another piece of the puzzle, another obstacle to prepare for the ultimate night surf.

Both of those nights were hard, and they caused me a lot of anxiety, but they also gave me a sense of accomplishment and confidence. I knew that I could overcome my fear and just be in the moment.

Steve White once told me an ancient Taoist story called "Lion Lion" that perfectly explains the idea of being fully present and entering into the moment.

There is a man walking through the jungle, and he hears the roar of a lion behind him. The man gets frightened, and he frantically runs through the bushes. He's looking over his shoulder, and the sound continues to get louder and louder. He hears the footsteps of the lion approaching, and the roar gets louder and louder. He can almost feel the breath of the lion on the back of his neck, then just as he comes through the bushes, he ends up on the precipice of a cliff.

The lion is right behind him, and just in time the man scurries down the edge of this cliff holding on to two vines. The lion is right above his head pawing at him, trying to get to this man, so he scurries down a little bit lower, and just for this moment, he feels like he's safe.

The man continues to climb down the edge of this cliff, holding on to the two vines, but as he looks down he sees another lion below him. The lion below him is pacing back and forth, waiting for him to come all the way down the cliff. Now the man doesn't know what to do. He can't go up to the top of the cliff, but he can't scurry down to the bottom, either, and so he decides to just hang on and hope the lions will disappear.

As the man is holding on to these two vines, he starts to feel something gnawing and nibbling on the vines. He looks up, and there's a white mouse nibbling on the vine in his left hand, and he's thinking, *Oh great! Now what am I going to do? If this vine breaks, I'm only going to have this one other vine in my right hand to hold on to.*

He looks down at the lion below him. The lion is pacing back and forth staring up at the man, and then all of a sudden he feels something gnawing and nibbling on the vine in his right hand. He looks up and there's a little black mouse nibbling on the vine just next to him.

So now the man has a lion above him, a lion below him, a white mouse nibbling on the left vine, and a black mouse nibbling on the right vine. The man does not know what to do, and in that moment of fear and desperation he looks over to his side and he sees a beautiful, juicy peach. So he holds on to the vine, reaches over, grabs the peach, and takes a big, juicy bite.

The story of the lions is a metaphor of life.

The first lion is the lion of our birth—it is continually chasing us. The second lion is the lion of our death, waiting for us to come all the way down to the bottom of the cliff. The white mouse represents daytime, and the black mouse represents nighttime. Together they represent time, in general. When the man looks over and sees the juicy peach, that is a metaphor for being in the present moment. When the man reaches out for this most beautiful peach and takes a bite, he negates the lion of birth and the lion of death, and he negates the white mouse and the black mouse by entering into the moment, and in the moment, nothing else exists.

When Steve White told me that story, it felt very familiar for a little boy who once dove into the water after a peach before he knew what fear was. We're born without knowing fear, but somewhere along the way, we're taught what fear is. To succeed, we must teach ourselves how to manage that fear in order to stop it from controlling our lives.

For me, whether I was on a big wave, or free-diving, or training, I had to learn to manage my fear and focus on being in the present moment. My life and the success of my Big Wave depended on it. So does yours.

EXERCISE: OVERCOMING YOUR FEARS STEP BY STEP

Working through each fear step-by-step is the key to success. You can digest the information in smaller amounts, so you don't get overwhelmed. When people try to toss themselves straight into the deep end and tackle an issue full-on, there are so many unknowns that the problem becomes incomprehensible. But if you break it down and do it in manageable pieces, it is easier to work through and overcome.

For example, let's say your Big Wave is to do a TED Talk and you've done all the research on how to apply, how to prepare, and when and where the next TED Talk will be. You've done the groundwork, been accepted, and even written your talk! But you have a crippling fear of public speaking that's making you want to cancel and miss out on this big opportunity. What do you need to do?

1. Make a list of each of your fears (example: public speaking).

2. For each fear, break it down into smaller parts. (Public speaking involves 1. Being seen, 2. Speaking in front of an audience, 3. Being seen as an expert, 4. Engaging and educating the audience.)

3. Practice each one of these until the fear no longer holds power over you. Perhaps you're most terrified of speaking in front of an audience. A great step might be to enroll in a local Toastmasters International club where you'll learn how to speak well in front of a group. Or maybe you can start by reading books to children in your local library and learning how to interact with them and have fun.

There are always ways to overcome the obstacles and fears in our lives. Do one thing at a time and fully understand each step. Once you understand the first step, make sure you fully understand the next step, and so on. If you skip through one and two, then you're going to have a problem at three. If you accomplish steps one and two, and three is a little shaky, keep trying until you can execute it perfectly. It might take you longer than the guy who skipped through two and three, but when the shit hits the fan, if you are both at 10 but he skipped his way through, and you took twice as long to get there but you know your stuff back to front, the other guy's chains are going to snap because there will be tension on the areas he took shortcuts on. He won't have full control of what is going on—but you will.

CHAPTER 8

STEP #6: CREATE THE
PERFECT CONDITIONS

Waves are toys from God.

— CLAY MARZO

Why Jaws? What's so special about that wave anyway? When we first started talking about the Night Rider idea, I thought about doing it on a big wave in Mexico, or a big-wave spot in West Australia back at home. But one wave had a bigger reputation than others. The scariest wave of them all was Jaws. It would require all I had. Nothing about the wave, the cliff, or the boulders in front of it was easy, and if I could actually ride that wave at night, I knew that there wasn't a shadow of a doubt that I would have done something great.

Once we had the location picked out, we got the external conditions in place, including the plan, the tools, and the team. As for the other external conditions—that wasn't easy, and we pretty much just had to hope for the best. The perfect weather conditions required for Night Rider—a big wave, light winds, and a full moon for light—hadn't shown up in 10 years.

Once the whole vision was clear and everyone knew what they had to do to support the team, we then had to focus on staying in that state of readiness, making sure that everyone was keeping themselves in check, just in case the right conditions showed up. We'd all put in so many hours and dollars to make this work. If the perfect conditions had shown up and we weren't prepared, that would have been terrible. We knew we had to stay ready.

And all the while, I needed to focus on creating the perfect *internal* conditions for success. Most of the required conditions for a project like this were internal rather than external, and I'd been working on my internal conditions ever since I met Steve White. Internal conditions—at least for me—were things I could control, such as my mental strength, my physical conditioning, my ability to hold a six-minute-plus breath underwater, and the assurance that we'd covered every possible obstacle I might encounter.

While we were waiting for perfect weather, I worked to make sure that I was clear on all levels, that I had everything in check, and that I was not taking any shortcuts, like I had been doing when I'd been injured.

ASSESSING THE LIMITATIONS

While most limitations are internal (faulty beliefs and old stories), some limitations are real. For example, I needed to execute Night Rider while I was still young and strong and healthy. If I had waited until I was 55 years old to do such a dangerous project, I doubt the results would have been in my favor.

I didn't want to end up wishing I had done it, but never having put in the effort of actually doing it. On top of not experiencing something so great, I'd have to tell my kids, "Yeah, I had this great dream, but I never followed through with it." That would teach them to quit, rather than to break through to success. I wanted to be able to say that even if I had failed, I had put everything I could into making it happen.

You need to assess whether your limitations are internal or external. And that is largely defined by what aspects you have the ability to control. Consider these questions in regard to your Big Wave and any limitations you'll need to consider:

1. Does your dream have a time limit?

2. Does your dream have an age requirement or age cutoff?

3. Does your dream require you to make unhealthy or impossible changes to your body?

4. Does your dream require the involvement of additional people?

5. Can you accomplish your dream in your current location, or does it require short- or long-term travel?

6. Does your dream require financial backing over and above what you have access to?

7. Do you have any disabilities, health concerns, or other issues that would require you to ask for outside help in accomplishing your dream?

8. Do you believe that you are worthy of doing something awesome with your life?

9. Do you believe that you were created with incredible capabilities?

10. Do you believe that you are creative enough to find a way to make your dream happen, even in the face of adversity?

INTERNAL CONDITIONS

Our "internal conditions" are the stories we tell ourselves. We first learned them as children when someone told us something about ourselves that we believed (even if it wasn't true), or perhaps it was something we learned by watching other people and internalizing their fears. We created these stories without understanding what we were doing, and they've been with us for years—decades even. So how we can make these stories work in our favor, instead of working against us? It can absolutely be done. Sometimes all it takes is a little rewording and rewiring to get us moving in the right direction.

Remember when I first met Steve White and saw those notes all over his house? He taught me that if I wasn't getting results that made me happy, I'd need to change my internal voices, since they drove my actions. I'd also have to make sure I reworded my voices in a positive way, rather than allowing any negative words to be imbedded by accident.

For example, let's say a parent doesn't want their kids to play on the road. The parent says to them, "Kids, get off the road!" But all the kids hear is "road." The directive "get off" assumes the kids are doing something negative by being on something they shouldn't be on, and negative instructions aren't usually something we want to listen to.

To be crystal clear on the intentions, the parent should reword the command to: "Kids, stay on the sidewalk." There is no "road"; the words that the kids hear are *sidewalk*. And the words *stay on* indicate that they're moving in the right direction, not doing something bad. By being selective about which words we use, we can avoid the possibility of failure based on an incomplete understanding of the goal.

This wordplay was the same type of channeling I had to do in my head. If I were to say to myself while surfing, "Don't fall off," then in my head, all I can hear is "Fall off," because it's a negative directive. Instead when I caught those waves, I kept saying to myself, "Stay on your feet," which is a positive affirmation. It's an encouraging directive, and it produces a kind of mental chant of the outcome I wanted. I chanted it to myself every time I caught a wave. Being on a wave is such an intense moment, and instead of allowing my thoughts to flood my body with doubts and a million questions, I steadied my mind and just kept thinking, *I want this*. I said the outcomes I wanted, and it worked!

Based on my work with Steve White, I trained nearly as much with my mental abilities as I did with the physical, since the mental side is equally as important as physical endurance and agility.

As the time drew near for the Night Rider project to go live, I was stressed out and not sleeping great, so I would say to myself, "Let's just stay calm and get through the day." Every day I would get through the day and stay calm. At night I would wake up a sweaty mess with my heart pounding, but I would keep reassuring myself.

If you say, "Don't think of a pink elephant," then everyone thinks of a pink elephant. I had to be saying *exactly* what I wanted, or otherwise I would get what I *didn't want*.

I also had to limit my focus each day. Focusing on something that hadn't happened wouldn't change anything for me. I needed to just focus on what was happening right now. I would purposefully tell myself, "I'm thinking about what is going to happen in five days, but what have I got to do right now? Right-o, I've got to go to training right now. I need to do this right now in this exact moment." I had to always try to be in the moment or my mind would spin out of control.

My coach Greg Dolman would say, "If you are ever too far in your head, thinking about future things that you can't control, you have to earth yourself." He meant I had to literally walk barefoot on the grass and feel what grass blades felt like on my feet. I had to walk over to the beach and feel what sand felt like on my toes. If I was feeling what that felt like, then I was in the "right now." If I started worrying about the future, Greg would tell me, "Go and tell me what grass blades feel like," and when you know what grass blades feel like, you know you are in the "right now." When you are in the "right now," you just have to focus on what you have to do *right now*. It sounded really funny to me at the time, but it worked. I also worked a lot with kinesiology.

TOOLS FOR EMOTIONAL CONDITIONING: KINESIOLOGY

Physical conditioning can get you far, but it can't get you all the way—at least not if you want a well-rounded and healthy result. To be healthy—body, mind, and spirit—you need to work on your emotional conditioning too.

My strength and conditioning coach, Greg Dolman, was also a kinesiologist. He trained a woman who was the five-time body-sculpting World Figure champion, purely through kinesiology, through tapping into her body and how her neural system responded and what she needed to do for training and nutrition. She won five World Figure titles from purely doing that, which is pretty damn impressive.

So what's kinesiology anyway? Let's imagine you want to build a house and you need help with building the structure (the body). So you work with a personal trainer, who builds the structure of the body. The kinesiologist is the electrician for the house. They make sure the wiring is functioning properly and that there are no blockages or tangles in your wiring.

We all store fears and mental anguish in our body. We also store emotional experiences—both good and bad. So, say something happened to you when you were younger and it really pissed you off. You have stored that event and the accompanying emotion somewhere in your body. When a kinesiologist goes to work on your overall structure, they would say something like, "You've got a massive block in your right knee."

You would say, "I had an injury there years ago."

They would tell you, "It has something to do with your dad when you were 14," and then you remember the time you and your dad had a fight about something and you were playing soccer in the backyard and this injury happened. You feel it as a *physical injury*, and a kinesiologist can relate it back to an *emotional injury* that is stored in your body that is now a blockage and stops you from functioning normally. I'll be honest, the fact that a kinesiologist can even pull that up scared the shit out of me the first time it happened!

But the longer you work with a kinesiologist, the more you understand just how connected our emotional and physical experiences are. The good news is that once you've isolated and acknowledged a particular blockage, you can work to get rid of it. The kinesiologist might talk to you about it and say, "If you were to go back there now, understand it from this different point of view." They give you the knowledge to deal with it. It's like understanding the incident from every angle, and using that clarity to understand how to break down your fear. You are then able to analyze it as an adult and understand it for what it is, which is brilliant!

Suddenly you let go of that offense because it makes sense. As soon as you understand it, you let go of it, and you rid yourself of all these things you are holding on to. Kinesiologists refer to it as "dis-ease" in your body, like you have a disease—and over time, if you don't release all this shit, it can become a literal disease. Some say the actual clinical breakdown of cancer is the buildup of negative emotions over time.

My kinesiology work with Greg is really based on neuromuscular response (which he calls BodyTune, or BT). As Greg says,[1]

> Kinesiology requires (generally) to have an extended elbow or shoulder that the practitioner uses to "talk" to the client's body by communicating with the body's

innate wisdom, with a strong muscle response meaning *no* and a weak response meaning *yes*.

BT is used by just touching the client's arm, hand, leg, or foot, and is gentler for the client; it doesn't require me to have a strong or weak muscle response from the client.

When we trust our gut feelings (intuition), we are listening to our innate wisdom which guides us to what is best for us at that time of testing. My process has allowed me to train champions in four different sports, from state, to national, to world champion status. So I know what I do is different from many other fitness professionals, but it works very well when we all trust our "gut."

The first goal that Mark and I faced when we started working as a team was to sort out his physical imbalances and relate how his emotional imbalances were related. Mark was having reoccurring injuries before I came on the scene. This is how I came to be involved with Mark. A mutual friend/client told Mark that he needed to see me as I would be able to sort out his injury and the cause, which would alleviate any further injury.

Once we started the process and Mark was noticing the improvements on all levels of his body, he started to have even more faith in the process I brought to his training protocols.

The BT method can be used for any issue that a client has. Muscular aches and pains, emotional issues, and being unable to make decisions and break life patterns that aren't productive—these are just a few of the challenges in my work with clients. A BT session will give the client clarity around their situation so that a way out of a situation is easier to resolve with 100-percent faith in their decision.

I worked with a kinesiology coach for years, learning how to unload the emotional buildup of different events and stressors. But at first I was skeptical. Being a typical man, I thought I didn't have a problem. Why would I need help? Greg explained to me that when something pissed me off or there was something I was frustrated with, yeah I could just shake it off and go on, but I'd still store it in my body somewhere. That causes an emotional block, and down the line, those things can cause injuries.

It all sounded like bullshit, but once I actually started working with a kinesiologist I found it to be true. He would do muscle testing, and would uncover a lot of limiting beliefs I had as a kid. He would say, "Did you have an issue with your dad or something when you were younger?" We would uncover it until I understood that there is a reason I had a certain habit now, that it was because of something I took on as a kid.

> **CASE STUDY: CANVA (WWW.CANVA.COM)**
> In July 2012, Melanie Perkins, Cliff Obrecht, and Cameron Adams launched Canva, an easy-to-use graphic-design program that allows people to make beautiful designs without in-depth knowledge of typical design programs. Today more than 10 million people use Canva, and it's been touted as "the easiest design program to use in the world," according to The Webbys.

I'd have to think of that situation and explain it to him, and then I'd look at it from an adult's point of view, with a rational mind, and I would realize that it was not worth harboring this frustration anymore or continuing to be mad at someone for something I was still carrying years later. Basically, I was walking around with this bag of emotional shit that I didn't really need to be hauling around with me. Once I started offloading all that stuff, I had room to bring on new things that I wanted to do. It was a type of self-healing. But I needed to do it over and over again, because we are all just carrying so much.

Say an interaction with someone annoyed me, and I said, "This is bullshit; what a wanker." Me leaving it at that is me storing it somewhere. A week later I'm about to snap about something because I have all these little issues that I've stored for no reason. Then I realize that it is not important. I need to forgive that person so that I can rid myself of that weight.

In my work with Greg, I realized I carried so many fears of setting a goal and not achieving it, and that stemmed back to a time when I was younger and I wanted to do something but felt uncertain or incapable. To be honest, once I cleared myself of all these things I had been carrying for years, I became really good at identifying things on my own and then getting rid of them.

Every time I was injured, we would always go into the reason why, and what the blocks were, and what created that whole injury in the first place. My gym coach is a kinesiology coach, so when I am in gym training, I do muscle testing on what I am going to do before I start training—what my body says I want to do, not what my mind or ego says I want to do. I found that when I don't have these extra things on my mind, if I'm focused on clearing excess emotions, I started becoming more of a whole person.

In a way, it feels as though kinesiologists are part therapists, part doctors, and part physical therapists. They teach you to help yourself. They are not telling you anything you don't already know, but they are tapping into your subconscious mind. Your mind will say rational things and your subconscious mind or soul will say truth. In your heart you will know right from wrong, but sometimes your mind can try to justify things you know aren't right for you.

A good friend of mine passed away last year from cancer, and some close relatives have also died of cancer. They were people who often weren't very open about their feelings, and they kept their emotions bottled up for decades. I'll always wonder if there wasn't a direct connection to holding on to emotions and the cancer that finally stole my good friend's life, as well as the lives of my relatives.

Now, I understand this is a very out-there way of thinking, and you can choose to believe it or not. But after learning the science behind it and seeing the results in my own life, it is something that resonated with me. It made sense. When certain things were brought up—whether they were disagreements I'd had with someone, a misunderstanding, or an instance where I felt I was wronged—and then I was able to understand it differently, sometimes even from the other person's perspective, and let it go, I always felt lighter. I felt like I was moving burdens I was storing. And it helped me to clear not only my mind, but also my body of dis-ease.

TOOLS FOR EMOTIONAL CONDITIONING: EMOTIONAL FREEDOM TECHNIQUES (EFT)

Through my work with Greg, I also learned about Emotional Freedom Technique (EFT) tapping, which is a form of counseling therapy. It's based on several theories of alternative medicine, including acupuncture, neuro-linguistic programming, energy medicine, and Thought Field Therapy (TFT). This is a very powerful tool, and it is something I use all the time. All it entails is literally tapping with your fingers on specific parts of your body— the same meridian points used in acupuncture—to release blockages that have created negative emotions.

The guide I've used most often is one I found online called "Gary's Courses: Online Coaching Library."[2] It's helped me eliminate negative energy and accept myself for who I am. If I have an issue with something, Greg will say, "Mate, you need to go tap that shit out tonight." Of course, if I told any of my friends I was doing it, they would think I was a weirdo, but I know now that it works, and it has helped me so much.

EFT also encourages positive affirmations as you're doing the tapping. For example, some of mine have been:

- "Even though I have this fear of completing the Night Rider project, I deeply and completely love and accept myself."

- "Even though I have this fear I'm not worthy of taking on Jaws at night, I deeply and completely love and accept myself."

- "Even though I have this feeling I can't do everything I've dreamed of doing, I deeply and completely love and accept myself."

- "Even though I have this feeling I am not worthy of everything that is rightfully mine, I deeply and completely love and accept myself."

By doing this routine, you are okay with being you, and you feel good about it. You take away the anxiety of all these things you want but are not quite sure you can have. When you remove the anxiety and fear, you are no longer blocked from having what you want.

EXERCISE: Recognizing and Working with Your Emotional Baggage

I'd bet that every single person carries some emotional baggage. It's a part of life—we have all been offended, frustrated, hurt, angry, sad, and more. We can't always prevent those feelings, but we can decide what to do with them. Will we hold on to them and carry them around with us? Or will we release them and choose to be healthy and happy?

Here are some questions to ask yourself as you begin to unpack your emotional baggage:

1. Am I regularly taking the time to uncover and work through my emotional stress?

2. When I engage in this process, do I feel a sense of relief, or do I feel anxiety?

3. Am I ready to leave behind old patterns that do not serve me?

4. Am I able to forgive the people and the events in the past that have hurt me in some way?

5. Do I still carry anger toward someone or something?

6. If so, do I experience that anger as a physical feeling—either as a headache, indigestion, muscle aches, or insomnia?

7. Have I forgiven myself—not for the painful things that have been done to me or that I have experienced, but for holding on to the negative emotions ever since?

8. Do I believe that I deserve to experience freedom in my emotional life?

9. What modes of self-care and self-love do I regularly engage in?

10. Can I find several things *each day* to be thankful for and celebrate?

Make a list of any areas of self-care that you're currently involved in. This could be anything from regular massages, therapy, EFT, and kinesiology, to yoga, meditation, journaling, or primal scream therapy. (Yes, there's such a thing.) If you aren't currently involved in any form of self-care, make it your job to find something that works for you.

CHAPTER 9

STEP #7: KNOW THAT SHIT WILL STILL GO DOWN

Surfing is attitude dancing.

— GERRY LOPEZ

We finally got the call to get ready. One week before Night Rider happened, we saw the swell coming; the forecast said the waves were going to be 65 feet high. It was going to be a huge, huge swell! I knew without a shadow of a doubt that *this* was the swell we were going to take. The question was, could I ride a swell that big at night?

In the swell prediction forecast, we could see where the storm was coming from. Sometimes when swells pop up out of nowhere and they are six days out, there is a fair chance they'll lose their power before they hit land. But when there is a big one and it is coming from Japan to Hawaii, then it usually tends to stack up the way we think it will—the way we needed it to.

This one was coming from Japan. I had spoken to a lot of the big-wave surfers in Hawaii, and they were all saying, "Oh yeah, this one is looking real big." There was no question on the size of this swell. It was going to be solid.

The day after we got the initial call, I began waking up every morning at about 5 A.M. in a panic, heart pounding, stomach aching, anxious, and sweating. *Holy shit, something big is going down real soon.* By 5:30 A.M., I was pacing around my house, just waiting for the day to hurry up and be over, because I was so anxious and nervous. It was really, really intense. I kept trying to distract myself. I wanted all the other distractions of my normal life to take over so I could maybe get myself in a different headspace. I wanted the phones on, and I wanted noise to be made to block out what was going on in my mind.

At that point in the process, we had already done all the preparation. All the gear was in place. It was just a matter of locking in flights and getting all the final things sorted, while still keeping the Night Rider project a secret.

Three days out, the swell was still solid, though it did back off a little bit. Now it was going to be more like 50 feet high with the occasional 60-foot set. The team got together and agreed: we are already confirmed, and we are definitely going.

We needed to fly to Maui immediately. I knew that all these other pro surfers would be flocking to Jaws, also known as Jaws, to try their luck at one of the most feared waves, not to mention one of the biggest rideable waves in the world.

If everything went right, I was going to be able to achieve my lifelong dream—achieving something that everyone else thought was impossible. No one had ever attempted to officially surf big waves at night, and certainly not Jaws. Smaller waves at night had proven difficult enough in the beginning of our project. But we'd worked through all the kinks we could. And we'd done a lot of testing in bigger surf, as well, just not as big as Jaws.

We were working with two different forecasting teams, including a guy named Ben McCartney, who runs Australia's biggest surf-forecasting website, called "Coastal Watch." He is one of the best forecasters in the world, and he's predicted some crazy things where I thought, *No way is this going to happen*, and considered not going out, but out of curiosity, I thought I'd have a look and see if he was right—and sure enough he was.

Ben has made predictions that were so specific. He's told me things like, in a certain spot in Western Australia, at 4:00 P.M. you are not going to see any waves, but by 4:30, there are going to be sets rolling in. Make sure you are out there from 4:30 onward. And he's always been right! I had a lot of faith in his forecasting skills.

There was another guy called Pat Caldwell who works in Hawaii, and he is quite famous for always getting the right calls on swells. Like if the big surf websites say, "It's going to be this and that," Pat will turn around and say, "It's going to be something else," and he's always right.

I wasn't married then, but Jacqueline and I were engaged (she is now my wife and mother of our lovely baby girl). She's from Western Australia, around Perth. When I met her, she knew what I did for a job. She had been surfing and would go a couple of times a year for fun—but she wasn't a hard-core surfer chick. Honestly, I liked that, because surfing was *my* space. I had previously dated people who really loved surfing, but I wanted to go and just surf the waves *I* wanted. If I had someone else with me, I was always being courteous and I'd end up surfing somewhere I didn't want to go. Whereas Jacqueline was happy for me to do what I wanted to do. It worked out better because when I came back from surfing, I was really pumped to spend time with her.

In fact, while I was dating Jacqueline, when I started working on the Night Rider project, I made her sign a nondisclosure agreement (we laugh about that now). I don't think she understood exactly how dangerous it was, because she didn't understand surfing at a really high level, but I reassured her that I knew exactly what I was doing, and she saw that I had put in so much work. She listened to the plan, asked questions about the details, and once I broke it down for her into those small steps, she thought it seemed very manageable. Her confidence in my training and preparation for the worst was so reassuring. She didn't think I seemed crazy, just calculated and careful.

It was so good that she and I were on the same page as a couple. It's such a key thing in life, that you, your partner, your business partner, your friends, and your work colleagues are all on the same page. If she had been terrified that I was going to die all the time, I would go home and see that in her eyes or feel that in the way she was acting toward certain things. But she was calm, and that helped me be calm.

As for my parents, I didn't tell them everything. They are older, and they have some limiting beliefs. Their visions for me early on weren't for me to become a surfer. It came from a place of love, but they wanted me to be an apprentice and get a "real job," or a "safe" job. I knew they wouldn't really comprehend what I was doing or why. And as much as I love my parents, I didn't want them offering suggestions or nagging me, when I had such a great team going over everything.

They didn't need to worry about me. They knew I was going to Hawaii to ride a wave at night. I even had to explain to them what it was afterward so they could understand that it wasn't something like going for a walk in the park. They didn't know a lot of the details until they saw the footage later.

So when our team made the call, we headed to Hawaii three days in advance to set up and do final preparations. I'm so glad we went above and beyond in our SWOT analysis, thinking of backup plans and solutions for everything that could go wrong. Because two days before the big swell came in, something did.

PREPARE FOR THE OPPORTUNITY

We waited 4 years for perfect weather conditions that hadn't come around for 10 years. A month before the perfect swell came in, another came up, and we wondered if that was the one. Five or six days out, we were all on standby, and then when it got to that three-day period where we could see what was happening, the conditions were changing and it was very much a 50/50 call, or a 60/40 in favor of it not being ideal, and we had to say, "Right-o, we are just going to have to wait for the next one," knowing very well that there might only be two swells that year.

November through February is your window for Jaws, but anything could happen in there. Some years there might be just one average swell, and some years there might be like 10 really good ones. You just don't know, because it depends on the weather system and whether it's going to be a linear pattern or an El Niño pattern. If there is an El Niño weather system, it will likely be a year of big waves.

During the days before Night Rider, I would go out during the day and test the boards that I was going to use that night—real high-speed stuff, even in small waves or flat water, because I knew I could actually test out how the boards would handle flat water going really, really fast on a Jet Ski, up to 90 kilometers an hour. That was a way to really gauge whether they could turn or handle chops and bumps.

A lot of people say you can never test out a big-wave board unless you are actually in big waves, and that's true to an extent, but I found that a lot of tests could give you some form of confidence in how the board would handle or react to certain things by just going really fast in rough conditions. I did a few tests and made sure I had all the straps right, and I wanted to make sure that when I put all the equipment on, there wasn't going to be anything I was surprised by on that particular night.

I wore the "exact game-day kit"—the exact type of short-leg, short-arm wetsuit; the specific light vest with the same switches and buckles; and the exact same surfboard I'd be using with the exact same straps—and ran drills over and over just so I was confident and so that on the night of the ride, nothing would feel unfamiliar. In the surfing world, that kind of preparation is just not something that people do—instead we usually figure it out on the day. That's what surfing's all about; you go out and test your board. You test your equipment, and you learn from those experiences. But we needed to know with certainty how our equipment would work under those conditions. That was something I was really drawing on to get an extra element of confidence.

Some surfers will purposefully tell themselves things like, "Don't worry about it; there is a fair chance that we are not even going to go out because of these factors," to help themselves be calm the night before. That is actually a good thing, because when you wake up, you can only deal with what is in front of you. There is no way to predict nature, so I actually think that's a really smart thing to do. But on this one, I was like, "It's definitely not going to be too small or too big." As it turned out, it was on the fringe of being too big but tapered off just enough to qualify as "as good as it gets." I had no way of dodging out of it.

WHEN THE SHIT HITS THE FAN

We weren't able to fly our own Jet Skis over, so we planned to rent three from a local shop, though we knew that we could get away with just one if we had to.

What we didn't want to do was alert anyone to exactly what we were doing—we were trying to fly under the radar a little, just rent the skis and do our own thing. But that was where shit went wrong again.

We had gotten two Jet Skis by now and were ready at the boat ramp to go out that day for a practice run. One of the production crew rang up the Jet Ski company to ask about an extra one, and instead of keeping the project quiet, this guy said, "Hey, I'm one of the producers from the Night Rider show."

The manager at the rental place said, "What Night Rider show?"

The producer continued to hype up who he was and what we were doing, making it sound like a bigger deal than it was. The manager was quiet for a few seconds, then said, "We are picking up all our Jet Skis now." The manager, realizing that this was a very risky project, refused to allow them to be rented because he was worried his Jet Skis would be smashed into a million pieces on the bottom of the cliff.

It was a total nightmare! We were getting ready, prepping, and then all of a sudden, everything was taken away from us. There we were, having flown our whole entire team here, and we'd been planning this thing for four years. It was three o'clock in the afternoon, and we were planning to ride out to Jaws around 2 A.M., in less than 12 hours.

That was a massive pain in the ass because, for once, we didn't have a plan B. We'd gone in six months earlier to organize everything to make sure we wouldn't be stuck without a Jet Ski and have to rely on someone to bring us one. We thought we had this locked down.

But instead of giving up, people started coming up with good ideas. Someone said, "I remember seeing a Jet Ski for sale on the way to our house where we are staying," and then we all thought we could get together all the money between us, and go purchase this Jet Ski.

So we went and did it. We could still go ahead with the mission. As a team, we had stuck together and found a creative way to make it work.

We decided that to be really smart and thorough, we needed to test the Jet Ski and make sure the person who would be driving that night had experience and was comfortable with it. Our original driver got cold feet and pulled out of the project at the last second, giving the excuse that he had to be on another island and couldn't make it. So we went to our plan B, using my brother Kevin as the backup driver. He was more than capable and had driven in a lot of big-wave spots all around the world. He'd done a training run out at Jaws the evening before, but he hadn't spent a lot of time in that particular wave, which was a possible risk. That wasn't an ideal situation for any of us.

I took Kevin out to test the ski, and he decided it felt safe. We pulled back in at about 5 p.m. and it was already starting to get dark because it was wintertime in Hawaii.

I was undoing the bungs on the back of the Jet Ski, which stops the water from going into the Jet Ski, and water just started pissing out the back of it. That didn't look good. I was looking around for what the problem could be. I said to the guys, "Last night it did rain a lot, so maybe it is just fresh water inside it." I tasted the water and it tasted a bit salty; it was hard to tell. So we drained all the water out and decided to put the Jet Ski back in the water, do a couple of loops, and test it again.

Kevin tested it and brought it back, and as I was undoing the bungs again, it pissed out even more water. The Jet Ski that we had just bought was full of tiny pinholes you couldn't see!

At that point I was losing my patience, thinking, *If there was ever a chance to give up and quit, now is your chance.* You tried to resurrrect it and work together, and you just got leveled again. Either way, we had to take the Jet Ski back.

At this point, I was both pissed off and anxious. We only had a few hours before the event, and we needed the helicopter pilot to stay with us. We also needed Jet Skis immediately.

As I was standing at the boat ramp, packing up the ski to return it, this guy I knew and liked, Yuri Soledad, happened to see me. Yuri is a champion big-wave surfer, and he lives in Maui. "Hey, Mark," he said. "It's good to see you. If you ever need me, here's my number. Give me a call." And that was it, which is still pretty amazing if you knew how rare and unexpected this offer really was.

Big-wave surfers don't usually offer too much help to other teams when there's a big swell and everyone flies in to town, because they're trying to sort their own stuff out. Yuri also doesn't usually give out his number, because if he did, people would ring him all the time. It was random seeing him there, but I took his number and didn't think much of it, since I was consumed with figuring out what to do about our Jet Ski problem.

As we were driving the Jet Ski back, I was thinking that this project was done. There was no way we could move forward because the ski was leaking, it was now dark, and we couldn't get a new ski to test it in time. There were all these reasons why it couldn't happen. "Everything is crap and fucked," was what I kept telling everybody.

I was supposed to surf just a few hours later, at 2 A.M. that night! The helicopter pilot was going to let us know by 9 P.M. if he could commit to coming. And then we were supposed to confirm that we were 100 percent in, as well.

When we got home, I was really frustrated since I was supposed to be focusing on surfing, and I'd taken on too much by trying to help out in other areas. My team saw that, and they told Jacqueline, "Take Mark over here, get him sidetracked, and get him out of this space right now."

Instead of following me in my frustrations, the team asked: What can we do? Are we done? Do we have to stop now? Is there nothing else we can do? They decided to contact someone else who had a Jet Ski for sale to see if we could rent it for the night and test it to make sure it was working properly. So they kept working on the side, away from me since I was too overwhelmed. A good team will know when someone is about to break and pull them out of a situation when it is necessary.

That great time made the project a success. The other team members were able to think calmly. They weren't completely mentally shot, like I was. They came up with a strategy and a plan. They had a couple of options for skis, and they got it all sorted. Without their initiative and leadership, we would have been screwed.

But then I remembered running into Yuri earlier in the day. I hadn't really mentioned what we were there for, but he'd said to call if I needed anything. And now it was a possible lifeline. We decided I should try him, even though in my head I was sure he would say no.

Yuri was a good friend. I knew him really well from being at big-wave events with him in Chile and Hawaii and other times when we'd chased swells around the world. We'd stayed together in Fiji, and he was a really good guy. But when you're surfing, you see guys that you know and you're like, "Hey, man, great to see you," but everyone is kind of on their own path or working with their own tight little group for that swell. After the swell comes, everyone is like best mates and more than happy to go have a beer or catch up for dinner, but normally leading up to it, everyone is kind of focused on their own game.

But on this day, I felt my intuition telling me I should call Yuri. I rang him and said, "Look, this is going to sound a bit weird, but I've been working on this project for years." I explained what we were going to do, and that we had all the safety crew ready, including a Special Forces commando, who had been practicing and strategically planning rescue drills the whole time, and I asked if he wanted to be involved.

Straightaway he said, "Yeah, I'm interested, and I've got a ski if you need it. I know that place like the back of my hand." He agreed to show up at Maliko Bay at 1:55 A.M., and we'd go over all the details. Unfortunately, there was a bit of a communication breakdown.

THERE'S ALWAYS ANOTHER ANGLE

I'd thought Yuri made it clear on the call that he wanted to be the main tow-in driver, but he thought he was being asked to be the main safety driver. I talked with Kevin after the call to Yuri, and told him that while I was confident in his abilities, Yuri said he was confident being the main driver and he was comfortable on his own Jet Ski. Kevin actually felt relieved. He knew he could get the job done, but he knew he wouldn't be as good a driver as someone who lived near Jaws year-round.

A few hours later at the bay, when Yuri realized we were expecting him to be the main driver instead of the main safety driver, he went along with it and stepped up again without question. We explained the plan to him in detail and if there was any hesitancy, we knew our backup plan (Kevin) was solid. But Yuri is an extremely competent person in that space, and he is amazingly skilled. He is one of the best big-wave surfers in the world. In 2016 he won the "Biggest Wave Award" for the biggest wave ever ridden at Jaws. While the Night Rider project was still a stretch for him, and definitely a challenge, if there was anyone I could choose, even going back, I would choose Yuri any day of the week. He was also a very humble guy and didn't have a big ego or a big macho presence about him, which was really crucial. I knew he'd make calculated decisions and he wasn't going to do anything reckless.

He didn't even tell us about the confusion until the next day!

Just after I called and asked Yuri to be involved, my guys came back with another Jet Ski they'd found. They'd already tested it and checked it underneath, and we now had all the skis we needed. Kevin would be on the second ski as the safety driver. It was 8:56 P.M., only four minutes before the call with the helicopter pilot to determine if we were all in. At 9 P.M., the helicopter pilot called us and said he was in, along with his backup chopper that would fly above him to protect him as well, and, thankfully, we could say we were ready on our end.

It was the biggest relief to have it all fall into place at the last minute, but I was mentally burned-out. I was overloaded with what was going down, and I was taking on too much. I was supposed to be staying calm and getting ready to be able to surf at night. It was going to be a long night, and I had to preserve as much energy as I could.

OVERCOMING OBSTACLES

Obstacles aren't dead ends; they're opportunities to be the best you can be. If someone says they have an obstacle, it shouldn't make them cringe. It should make them say, "Okay, how are we going to deal with this?"

From the very start of trying to do the Night Rider thing, we were laughed at. People were saying this was ridiculous, that we couldn't physically do what we wanted to do. When you're told that so many times, you become resilient. Honestly, it was so rewarding. Everything else in life is set up in a way now that when I hear no, it's almost funny. It's almost like a call to action. To me, an obstacle is a challenge to be the best I can be. How can I think of a new creative way to get what I want to do done? It's a puzzle that I enjoy solving.

I believe that when you're prepared, the universe works in your favor. I also find that when you are being true to yourself, you are never let down because you are doing what is right for you, and that always feels good. You can't tell me the guy who runs in his first marathon and finishes 200th, that he is going to be disappointed that he didn't win. No way! He's ecstatic that he gave everything he could to make his dream come true. For him, it's a lifetime achievement!

When obstacles come, and they will, they are testing how committed you are to finding another solution and working together as a team. In our case, obstacles were seen as challenges. They didn't stop the process or rule something out. They were constantly making us stretch or reach a little further or dig a little deeper, as a group and as individuals. This kind of stuff brings the best out of people.

And we needed the best from all of our people. Our abilities and determination would be tested in less than five hours.

EXERCISE: Overcoming Obstacles to Your Big Wave

In order to overcome your Big Wave, we're going to break down your obstacles into small pieces, just like we did with your fears. Once we do that, we can more easily manage each obstacle and find ways around them.

A friend of mine runs a successful multimillion-dollar business with his wife. When I asked about their success, they told me, "It's not the prettiest business in the world, but it wasn't until we understood every element of this business that we started to do it well. The reason we are doing well is because we have done every single part of it." When they first started, they were their own janitors and their own accountants, and they did every part of the business on their own, including the spreadsheets. They didn't like doing all of that, but they had to because they had no one else.

This paid off in the long run, because when you have an understanding of every single area of your business, you are able to know what is and isn't working properly. And once you're in a position to delegate to people who are more suited to those roles, you're able to operate to your strengths.

It would be easy to look at my friends with no knowledge of how they built the company from the ground up and say, "Oh, you are at the top end and you are just collecting checks." But they did all the little jobs along the way themselves, and that is why they understood their business so well.

The people who actually understand every single step and process will always run a business the most efficiently. Likewise, if you understand every step of your Big Wave, no matter how mundane, it will give you power and acceleration.

1. Make a detailed list of all the obstacles that will have to be overcome to make your Big Wave a reality.

2. Now that you have a list of your known obstacles, just like you did with the exercise on overcoming fear, break them down into smaller pieces. If your obstacle is finding 20 people who will help you fund your idea, some initial steps might be identifying those people based on location, income, or areas of interest. Another could be making sure you have a business plan in place.

3. For each small piece you've listed, give each one a timeline or a date of completion. This will make sure you maintain momentum.

EXERCISE: DEVELOP YOUR BACKUP PLAN

As you can see, both in my story and in your own life, things don't always go according to plan. We can't control Mother Nature, other people, or random shit that happens to us . . . but we can develop backup plans for each area of our Big Wave that could go wrong.

1. Make a list of at least 3 areas of your Big Wave where your plan could be upended by things you can't control.

2. Write out a plan B for each item.

3. Write out a plan C!

We never could have imagined our initial main driver getting pulled away on another assignment or that we'd buy a leaky ski. But we were thinking on our feet and we made plan B, and then plan C, and we went with it!

If you develop your backup plans, you can hopefully avoid getting caught in a situation like we did where you have to scramble to quickly come up with a solution.

CHAPTER 10

STEP #8: FOLLOW IT THROUGH TILL THE END

Only those who will risk going too far can possibly find out just how far one can go.

—T. S. ELIOT

There was always a risk that things could go wrong. And while the number of surfing-related deaths is relatively low compared with other extreme sports, it still happens, mostly when someone is knocked unconscious from wiping out or gets pummeled by a wave and then drowns. Others meet their misfortune if their leg rope becomes stuck between boulders or caught on the reef below and they are unable to get free in time. I never highlighted the exact details of this to my fiancée, Jacqueline. I figured it was important to keep her from worrying.

Of course, we had discussed all the possible outcomes. But once these were discussed, the fears were set aside, and the task was our focus. She saw the extensive training and the over-the-top preparation, so she knew I was taking the project seriously, above and beyond what was required. There would have been no point in focusing on what bad things might happen. We both needed to stay positive.

On the big night, she was there making sure everyone was eating and staying relaxed. She was helping the crew where she could, but also acting as a sounding board for me. It was an intense lead-up to the actual event, and I'm glad she was there to be my calm in the chaos, even though the guys filming were trying to get a rise out of her to add more drama to the documentary. The producer said to her, "Oh, you must be terrified knowing your fiancé could die at any time!"

But she was a pro. She turned around and looked at me and then him, and her response was spot-on. "No. He's going to make it look easy. He is fully trained and pre-pared for it."

He said, "Shit." Needless to say, that wasn't what the film guy was hoping for. It really pissed him off because he was trying to make her feel scared, which is a shithouse thing to do to someone's fiancée. But it was exactly what I needed.

When someone asked her how she felt about the ride, she said, "Mark is very calculated and prepares for all situa-tions. My confidence in his abilities far outweighs my fears, and I don't like to entertain the thought of death. I know big-wave surfing is a dangerous sport, and Night Rider is a dangerous event. I'm not naive, but if Mark didn't do what he loved, he would be like a caged animal. He would lose his spark. In the case of a complete tragedy, and Mark lost his life doing what he loved. . . . Isn't that living in itself?"

That's your dream wife right there.

Had she been panicky like the guys filming wanted her to be, that would have been devastating. She is a team member. Of all the people on the team, she had to be on the same page as me. Likewise, if another member of the team had been unhinged, it would tip the balance for the rest, and we all needed to be as calm as possible. At least on the surface. In my own head, I was still freaking out, just wanting it to be over.

In the months and years leading up to this project, I'd put myself through a range of intense physical demands and situations, overpreparing for every scenario my team could come up with. I didn't have any reference point in my training and preparations for what I did or didn't need to do. No one had ever done this before. My dive coach, Anthony, always said, "It's so much harder for the person who goes first." His thought was that when you go first, you figure it out for yourself, and you make the rules. Once you've done it, everyone else can just copy what you did.

On January 20, 2011, at 2 A.M. local time, the group was assembled—half at Maliko Bay and half on the cliff at Jaws. We had enlisted Maui's most experienced helicopter rescue team, and videographers, and Yuri and Kevin were there on the Jet Skis.

We'd checked and double-checked all the equipment, and now it was time to go. Jacqueline was on the cliff above, watching with the producer, some camera crew, sound tech, emergency response, a security guy, and a few friends, trying not to focus on her anxiety as she watched me disappear into the dark.

On the cliff, we had three blue-light beacons in certain trees that could reference where we were in the lineup so we would know which part of the reef we were actually on. Yuri had taken the lead tow-in driver role, and my brother was on the safety ski.

Speeding away from land, I had only a few minutes to think about what was about to happen. I wasn't panicked, but I'd be lying if I said I wasn't totally nervous. But we'd planned for everything. Checked all the equipment. Waited for the perfect conditions. And now we were ready.

A half-mile from the cliff, I got off the back of the Jet Ski. I climbed onto my board and grabbed the tow rope, and Yuri drove me into position to catch a wave. Within seconds I saw the stars disappear, and I was terrified as I heard the surge of the powerful water all around me. This was really happening!

I caught the first two waves hunched over in a survival stance on the board. On the third wave, I straightened up my back and instantly the waves lit up perfectly, illuminating the wall of water behind me. The red lights on the bottom of my surfboard glowed like fire as I cut through the black water.

The fourth wave was different—bigger and more powerful. I could feel it. My heart raced, and I focused my eyes on the shadows within the shadows. I worked to slow my breathing. And when I was able to feel what the board was doing, I was able to ride it and be fully present. All my senses were firing at once. It was like gliding down a slick mountainside, the board's fins cutting through the waves. In that moment, I was living that dream I'd been chasing for so long. The little boy of my childhood was all grown up, now one with the water.

The waves at Jaws were so big that Jacqueline and the rest of the crew could see them being lit up by the helicopters moving into position as they were standing on top of the cliff, overlooking the ocean. By that time, a few other surfers and onlookers had walked up to where the crew was standing, excited to watch as history was being made.

Everything was going fine—until the very end, when everything went wrong. The helicopter, looking for a better shot, sent its lights scanning across my face, instantly blinding me. Up until that point, my vision was fine. I had stayed in the dark, and my pupils remained dilated enough for me to see clearly. The only light I had been looking at was the red light at the bottom of my board, and that wasn't enough to affect my night vision. But with the lights of the helicopter shining on me, my pupils contracted, and I couldn't see anything at all.

Blinded, I didn't know where I was. Almost immediately I dived forward and wiped out. And I knew as soon as I hit the water that it was going to be one of the worst hold-downs I'd ever experienced. I didn't know if I was going to be picked up and slammed over the falls or what. It was purely the unknown, and I remember thinking, *Shit, what am I in for? This is not cool.*

Normally when you wipe out, you have a fair idea where you are and if there is a huge wall of water coming down on you. I was actually on the shoulder, which is the safest section of the wave.

Every wipeout is different. Sometimes you can get rattled to the point that you feel like your arms are getting pulled off your body. The force violently spins you around so hard and fast that your face and cheeks feel like they are getting ripped apart. Some people who have wiped out at Jaws have had their pectoral muscles torn off their chests. I wouldn't have believed it if I wasn't there when that happened, although that's an extreme result. It doesn't always end up that bad, but you are trying to be able to go with the energy and force of the wave that is whizzing you around.

But I couldn't move with the force of the wave, because I couldn't predict the way it was moving. I'd lost the last three to five seconds of vision when the light hit my eyes, so all I had to go on was feeling.

I was thinking, *I don't know where I am. I don't know what position of the wave was in front of me or behind me.* I just knew it was big enough to rattle the absolute crap out of my body. I saw blurs flying past my face underwater. I remember trying to just keep my head covered and go with it as much as possible.

CASE STUDY: SIR RICHARD BRANSON is an English business magnate, investor, and philanthropist, and his Virgin Group controls more than 400 companies. At the age of 16, his first company was a magazine called *Student*. He later opened a chain of record stores, airlines, and other businesses. In 2000, he was knighted at Buckingham Palace. Today his net worth is $5.2 billion.

From underwater, I could hear the sounds of Jet Ski engines roaring nearby. I had a big light on my back, so I literally would have been like a disco ball spinning underwater, but the light went out in the ferocity of what was happening. I think the force of the wave flicked the switch off, so they didn't know exactly where I was.

When I was down and spinning around, I was also wearing a glow stick on the back of my neck, just in case that exact thing happened, or if, for example, my light shorted out and they couldn't see me, they would see the red glow stick.

The pressure and intensity of the wave was so strong. When it finally let me go, I swam up to the surface to catch my breath and find the nearest Jet Ski. I put my hand up to touch air, but it turned out it wasn't air. I thought I had cleared the surface and tilted my head back to catch a big breath, but I sucked in a mouthful of water instead. I must have still been another foot or two underwater, but the water was so clear I couldn't tell it from the night air. I could see the stars so clearly, even through the water. Now I had just swallowed a heap of water, couldn't understand how that had happened, and was in desperate need of air. Despite my training, I wasn't staying calm.

I remember choking on the water, thinking, *What the hell is going on?*

The helicopter circled overhead, high beams boring into the foam below, searching for the red lights of my surfboard or for the light on the back of my vest.

I panicked and kicked toward the surface again; luckily my flotation vest pulled me up, and when I felt myself push through the top of the water, I coughed out the water and finally filled my lungs with fresh air.

Seconds after I surfaced, Yuri raced in to get me. He came around to my right side and yelled, "Get on!" As he shouted at me, I saw the stars vanish again, and I knew that a massive wave was about to crash right on our tail.

I screamed at him, "Just go! Go!" He gassed it without looking back and barely escaped being covered by another huge wave. I went underwater just as the wave hit, knowing I was doing what I had to do to get through the moment. We had trained for the worst-case scenarios, and we were right in the middle of one now.

When I went down that second time, although I was full of adrenaline, I wasn't as concerned about the next wave, because I knew it had already broken, which meant it had lost its power. It was still a big whitewash, but it wasn't going to be as bad as one that hadn't broken or one that could land on my head.

I finally surfaced between sets, and my brother Kevin charged in to pick me up while Yuri came out of the darkness and followed Kevin out to safety. Looking back, my time in the water felt like a half an hour, but I reckon it all happened in about five minutes.

I rode 14 waves that night before the safety crew called it off. The guys in the chopper were running out of fuel, and I felt like I'd been run over by a truck. I had wanted to keep going no matter what, but I was relieved when they made the call that I had to go in, because I felt like I physically couldn't do much more. It was the biggest relief to be riding back in, knowing that I'd done it and given it my heart and soul.

I stepped onto the boat ramp at Maliko Bay around 5 A.M. while it was still pitch black, having surfed for three hours straight. The team from the cliff was there to greet us and eager to hear about the experience, but I was speechless. It had been a real battle having the camera crew there; during much of the ride and the days leading up to it, they had become the enemy to me, always in my face and asking me to talk about things I didn't want to talk about.

I rode a roller coaster of emotions along with the waves that night. But now, having finished the ride, I was finally okay to talk to the crew, although I barely had a word to say. Jacqueline would later tell me that I was the quietest she'd ever seen me. Maybe it was the shock or disbelief that after all these years, I had finally completed what I had set out to do.

Back on dry land, I was just happy I was still standing and could still move my arms and legs. I felt like I could have gone and sat in a cane field and lain there for a week. I would have been totally content just listening to the wind blow. I was totally at peace with myself. I'd achieved my dream of surfing Jaws at night. And we'd done it as a team.

That morning, the swell had peaked at 4 A.M. according to the local weather report, and it would slowly drop off as the day went on. The sun came up at about 5:50 A.M., and just as we were finishing getting everything packed up, a bunch of eager surfers arrived. They were a little confused about how we could have already been out, but they had no clue what we'd just done. They gave us some sarcastic attitude, and I'm guessing they were thinking we'd put our skis in and then decided, "No, it's dark; we don't want to do it." Thinking we were over it, one of the guys said to us, "Too big for you, eh?"

I looked over and said, "Yeah, man, too big." I had a smirk on my face as I walked away, as did the rest of our team.

I sat in the cab of the truck as we drove off just quietly saying to myself, "Yeah, man, it's too big," and trying not to laugh. They'd find out soon enough what we'd just done.

We got home around 6:30, so the sun wasn't fully up but there was still a lot of light. Still on an adrenaline high, I was exhausted but too amped up to sleep. I was finally able to wind down around 11:00 that day, and I laid down to rest. But I only slept for like a half an hour.

That night we went to a bar to have a couple of drinks with dinner. Everyone was in complete celebration mode. It was such a good vibe. I was still much more quiet than usual, but oh so happy. I was numb and completely shot, having used every ounce of adrenaline in my body, but my daze was completely content.

The production crew had set up a press release that went out to the media just a few hours after we'd stepped off the beach, but the news stations and surf sites hadn't had time to report on it, so it wasn't public knowledge yet. No one knew what we'd done less than 24 hours earlier—it was like our little secret. We would get the group together two months later in Australia to properly celebrate, but for now we were just enjoying the accomplishment.

Early the next morning, I sent a picture to Micky
Maidens, a still from the film taken during my Night
Rider experience. (Video clips and stills from the ride are
now available at markvisser.net.) There was a Jet Ski to
the side of the frame, a helicopter in one corner, and a
full moon above, and I was surfing down a 40-foot black
wave with my light pack on my back and red lights under
my surfboard. It was an awesome shot, and I was thrilled
with it. Micky had a young family at home and hadn't
been able to make the trip to Hawaii to witness it in person—plus, he confessed to me that as much as he'd have
loved to be there, he would have been so nervous.

Almost immediately he sent me back a picture that
blew my mind. In the business plan, we'd had a watercolor
artist re-create my original drawings of how I thought the
lighting should be positioned, how the surfboard would
look, and what I'd be wearing. In this one drawing Micky
sent, the artist's drawing was *exactly* like the picture I'd
just sent him! There was a boat to one side of the frame,
a helicopter in one corner, and a full moon above, and
I was surfing down a 40-foot wave. Even stranger, the
artist had sent us his drawings three years earlier—to the
day—of the Night Rider event.

It was so eerily similar to reality that when I showed
my group, we all were silent for a bit, letting it sink in that
something we'd planned for so long had been re-created
almost exactly as we'd imagined.

It was proof—to all of us—not only that anything is
possible, but how powerful our intentions and imagina-
tions can be when we tap into them and use that creativity
and determination to drive us forward.

LET GO OF THE SPECIFICS

Once the moment of your Big Wave arrives, there is nothing to do but follow it through. And most likely, it's not going to happen exactly the way your original plan said. So let that go. Keep to your core values and your big vision, and you'll ride it out, no matter what the details look like.

After all the shit that went down—the Jet Ski fiasco and losing our original driver—I was still prepared and ready to go through with it. I was frustrated and anxious, but I knew there had to be a way. We hadn't been preparing for four years for nothing!

My team did what they do best, and I went into laser focus on what I had to do. I kept that focus the entire time I was on the water. First, I concentrated on being towed out. I told myself, "I've got to stay on my board the whole way until I get to the wave." Then when I got on the wave, I thought, "I just need to stay on my feet." I was never ahead of what was happening in that exact moment.

In the months leading up to the ride, in my head, I had this vision of what I thought riding a huge wave would be at night and how it would all feel, but I didn't really have a clue what it would be like until I was actually there. If I had spent my time thinking about all the scenarios that could have happened, it would have been exhausting, and I needed to reserve all my mental and physical strength. So I let go of any expectation of what it was going to be like, and I let go of trying to control the outcome. My mantra became: *Now it's time to be present right now and be in this moment, and it is what it is, because there is nothing that can change that.* And as it happened, reality was so much more amazing than anything I could have imagined.

Even with the obstacles I encountered on the first two waves when I was a bit scared and in the wrong standing position, the experience was still above and beyond what I had imagined it would be, even though it was the most terrifying thing ever. And then when I was able to really ride that wave and look over my shoulder and see what was around me, it became an incredible, beautiful experience.

Driving out there and catching the first wave, even with all the preparations and all the work we'd done, I still didn't know if it could work. There were so many questions in the back of my head, like, "Is this really actually achievable?" But after catching several waves and really being able to ride them, I had no more questions—there was just the moment, of looking up and seeing nothing but shadows and stars, and then bending around dark corners, the feeling of flying through the night.

WHAT ACHIEVEMENT FEELS LIKE

I knew I could use this experience for encouragement with anything else I ever wanted to do again in my life. If I could do *this*, I could do anything. And not only that— I felt like a lifelong burden had lifted. I'd been trying to prove something to myself for so long, and I was free of it now.

I achieved a deeper self-acceptance. I no longer needed to be the best big-wave surfer in the world. Night Rider humbled me to the point where I realized that all these things I'd been trying to do to prove myself to others (and to myself)—I didn't need to do them anymore. I only needed to believe in myself *and* believe that I was capable of doing amazing things and inspiring others.

For years I had carried this massive burden where I didn't believe I could do all these things I wanted to do. I didn't think I was worthy enough. As it turned out, that same doubt was why I was able to provide such a great example for others, because I am really just a normal person—and I really believed unless I completed this massive project, I was just going to be a normal person for the rest of my life. I didn't have advantages like money or connections or the Hawaiian upbringing. The only thing I had was my mind and my heart, and that's exactly what every single other person has. That is a gift we all have.

I knew I couldn't tell someone else to go running wildly after their own dreams without having first done it myself. I wouldn't have any credibility or influence. I needed to walk the walk. In every situation for the rest of my life, where I might be trying to help anyone else, I needed to be able to draw on my experiences and be able to say, "Yeah, I remember being in this exact situation. This is exactly what happened. I can tell you firsthand, because I lived it, and I am not some freakish god. I'm just the same as you."

Plus, anything else I want to do now, I know I will be able to use the exact same planning process and motivation that I had for the Night Rider project. Anything in my life that seems like a massive wave—like marriage or fatherhood—I can break it down in any way that I want. I can achieve whatever I want to achieve, because I've already done it.

Night Rider gave me a higher level of credibility as a professional athlete. But more important, it gave me a higher level of self-worth. If you are doing something in the public eye, you need credibility. But as an individual, all you really need is self-worth and self-love. Setting an example for yourself, proving to *yourself* what you can do, can help you grow enormously as a person.

Now, you don't have to put yourself through the same torturous obstacles that I did in order to achieve that. I look back and think, *Had I been interested in self-improvement sooner, or not procrastinated on the training, I wouldn't have had to beat myself up so much*, but knowing the role I believe I have for my life, which is to speak out and help others, I almost feel like I needed to have done it the hard way in order to be a more useful role model.

The reality is, you've got to love you for you. Before you accomplish anything amazing, I believe you have to focus on self-worth and self-love. And I can promise you— there's no feeling like the feeling of accomplishment.

CONTINUE TO ENCOURAGE OTHERS

Success can be a funny thing. When the press release went out the morning of the ride, the team was ready to spread the message of inspiration. And the stories that came in from viewers were amazing!

I heard some pretty humbling stories. One woman who saw me later at a keynote speaking event asked me, "How do you accept fear knowing you could have died?" The thing is, I never thought dying was a possibility. I had done all this training and I was prepared. But for this woman, fear controlled her life.

She explained that someone had held a gun to her head during a Russian war. She had crawled through a hole to escape, and now she lived in Australia. She said her whole life she had always been so fearful, because she thought that was a situation where she could have died . . . so how could she ever get over it?

For starters, I told her she was way more hard-core than me, because I'd never had anyone put a gun to my head and I hadn't had to crawl through a hole or escape a war, but at the end of the day, you can't worry about that kind of stuff. She was consumed by thinking she was going to put herself in a place where she was going to die, because in the past, someone could have ended her life. All I could tell her was that they hadn't and that she was still here for a reason. She hugged me and started crying.

Another guy said he was told he couldn't walk due to a spinal condition called neuropathy. Seeing Night Rider really inspired him to try physical therapy and overcome his fear, and now he was walking. Wow, how awesome is that? Normal people *can* do extraordinary things.

While 99 percent of the people were so ecstatic for us, for me, and for what our team had accomplished, there will always be the 1 percent who are bitter or pissed off that they didn't do something like this. Some people even complained that using a helicopter for our safety was wrong because it was polluting the air. But my sense is that deep down they're frustrated because they haven't achieved their own goals.

For those of you who are sensitive to criticism or who are worried about what other people will think of you, I can guarantee you that you will experience negative feedback. It's not a question of if. It's a question of when. And you can only protect yourself so much—you can be selective about who you share your Big Wave with, and you can purposely seek out team members and peers who will encourage you and celebrate you. You can avoid reading comments from the Internet trolls. But sometimes even your family or friends won't understand what you're doing, why you're doing it, or how to keep their mouths shut if they don't agree.

At the end of the day, you have to be okay with yourself, your reasons, and your worth. Screw what anyone else thinks! If you're not hurting anyone and you're following your dream, you can never worry about what anyone else thinks. Their opinions are none of your business.

It was amazing to see so many people who were actually moved by hearing about this project. That meant everything to me and that was what it was all about. I don't care if people know my name or not, but if they know what the project stands for, that's all that matters to me. This message is something that will outlive any individual, and that's exactly what I wanted. This type of work is what I want to do for the rest of my time.

Our own team was so moved by the success of the Night Rider project too. Those who were on the team felt an amazing sense of accomplishment, and that gave them confidence that they could use in every part of their lives as well.

A few weeks after the ride, Yuri and I were talking about it. He explained how he instantly became emotionally invested in the project, and how being involved changed his life forever. He told me, "Your dream became my dream. That is the most amazing thing I've ever done." It was something he would never forget. And since then he has become one of my best mates. I'm always with him every single time I go to Hawaii. He's become family. It's been that way ever since that night at Jaws, and I think it'll be that way for the rest of my life.

LOOK FOR THE NEXT BIG WAVE

People have said to me, "You've completed your life's mission, your big dream as a child, and you are not even in your mid-30s—so what is your next dream?" The truth is I'm working on another project already, which is probably the biggest project that I will ever achieve—or at least the biggest project my mind can currently comprehend. But in the meantime, I'm staying busy doing what I love—surfing and inspiring others.

I'm still a professional big-wave surfer and ocean adventurer. I won the ASL Big Wave Award for biggest "paddle in wave" for 2014–2015. I'm sponsored by many amazing brands, but I have strict rules about only working with companies that understand my message, have the same morals, and also want to inspire people to be all they can be. My role is still to capture exciting big-wave footage and tales of great adventures and to inspire others to do the same—whatever that means to them.

CASE STUDY: MICHAEL JORDAN turned his passion into his brand. Known as the greatest basketball player of all time, Jordan's prolific career has earned him numerous awards and accomplishments, including Olympic gold medals, five MVP awards, becoming the first billionaire NBA player in history, the world's second-richest African American, one of the most successful African American business owners in history, and endorsing Nike's Air Jordan sneakers.

I have been working on several film projects based on adventure, inspiration, and new perspectives. I'm also a keynote speaker on risk assessment, planning, and teamwork for corporate banks and large businesses and groups.

I'm honored to say I have trained the most elite Special Forces units in the world in underwater tactical drills, including the SAS in Australia, the Navy SEALs in America, and the Mexican Marines. I've worked with professional football teams. I have worked with Olympic teams. I developed and honed my skills to such a high level that I'm able to share that knowledge with others—everything I learned from big-wave surfing, and all that I have picked up along the way.

I teach a course in Fiji on a private island and another in the Bahamas called "The Ocean Warrior Course." We hold six classes a year, teaching everyday people about water safety. Whether they want to get into surfing and enjoy small waves, medium waves, or big waves, or whether they just want to be able to go for a swim in the ocean, we break down all the barriers and obstacles for someone who wants to be able to enjoy the ocean.

The more people in the world I can help, the better. I once had this vision of being the best big-wave surfer in the world, and that would have inspired a lot of people in the world of surfing, but it didn't feel right to me. When I decided that what I really wanted to do was inspire people all around the world to be the best they can be, that vision felt *right*. I was in the flow.

It feels so much more satisfying to have helped all types of people, not just people who want to do the sport that I love. I wake up every morning feeling pumped. The work I do gives me endless energy. Surfing is a trade of love that helps me fulfill my greater purpose, which is to inspire and help people.

When I think back to that little boy who dreamed of being a surfer, I see a young spirit full of life and wonder—but also hesitancy. That kid was so afraid of not being able to achieve his dream. I had so many fears and thoughts of, "I can't do it." I had such a fear of being normal and lost in the crowd of humanity that I thought I wouldn't be able to do anything special in my life. It took me 30 years to figure it out.

If I could say anything to that little kid, I would say, "Mate, don't fear all the things you fear. Whatever dream you have, you can do it. Even if other people tell you that you can't, it's only because they are afraid *they* can't achieve whatever they're dreaming of doing. But really . . . they can too."

I used to wish I was Michael Jordan. Today I can say with all honesty, I'm really grateful that I am me. I'm extremely happy with who I am, and I am totally content with my life and what I've achieved. I believe I am now on track with my true path, with much to learn and a worthy journey ahead.

But I still think Michael Jordan is really cool.

ENDNOTES

1. Interview with Greg Dolman, October 15, 2016.

2. Gary's EFT Coaching Library: Borrowing Benefits (Easy EFT), "Getting Started," http://www.emofree.com/gcl-borrow/Bb-started .html.

ABOUT THE AUTHOR

Mark Visser is an Australian big-wave surfer and ocean adventurer. He was the 2014–2015 Big Wave Paddle-in Champion and three-time runner-up for the ASL Big Wave Awards. Mark spends his time tracking down some of the biggest waves in the world utilizing innovative technology and pioneering unique ways to surf them. In 2011, Mark made history by achieving a night ride on 30- to 40-foot waves at the infamous Jaws break in Maui. Mark is a frequent motivational and corporate speaker and teaches courses on water safety. You can visit him online at markvisser.net.

Hay House Titles of Related Interest

YOU CAN HEAL YOUR LIFE, the movie,
starring Louise Hay & Friends
(available as a 1-DVD program, an expanded 2-DVD set,
and an online streaming video)
Learn more at: **www.hayhouse.com/louise-movie**

THE SHIFT, the movie,
starring Dr. Wayne W. Dyer
(available as a 1-DVD program, an expanded 2-DVD set,
and an online streaming video)
Learn more at: **www.hayhouse.com/the-shift-movie**

*ABUNDANCE UNLEASHED: Open Yourself to More Money,
Love, Health, and Happiness Now,*
by Christian Mickelsen

*CONSCIOUS COMMUNICATIONS: Your Step-by-Step Guide
to Harnessing the Power of Your Words to Change Your Mind,
Your Choices, and Your Life,*
by Mary Shores

*THE SACRED SIX: The Simple, Step-by-Step Process for
Focusing Your Attention and Recovering Your Dreams,*
by JB Glossinger

*SH#T YOUR EGO SAYS: Strategies to Overthrow Your Ego and
Become the Hero of Your Story,*
by James McCrae

All of the above are available at your local bookstore
or may be ordered by contacting Hay House (see next page).

We hope you enjoyed this Hay House book. If you'd like to receive our online catalog featuring additional information on Hay House books and products, or if you'd like to find out more about the Hay Foundation, please contact:

Hay House, Inc., P.O. Box 5100, Carlsbad, CA 92018-5100
(760) 431-7695 or (800) 654-5126
(760) 431-6948 (fax) or (800) 650-5115 (fax)
www.hayhouse.com® • **www.hayfoundation.org**

Published and distributed in Australia by:
Hay House Australia Pty. Ltd., 18/36 Ralph St., Alexandria NSW 2015
Phone: 612-9669-4299 • *Fax:* 612-9669-4144 • www.hayhouse.com.au

Published and distributed in the United Kingdom by:
Hay House UK, Ltd., Astley House, 33 Notting Hill Gate,
London W11 3JQ • Phone: 44-20-3675-2450 • Fax: 44-20-3675-2451
www.hayhouse.co.uk

Published and distributed in the Republic of South Africa by:
Hay House SA (Pty), Ltd., P.O. Box 990, Witkoppen 2068
info@hayhouse.co.za • www.hayhouse.co.za

Published in India by: Hay House Publishers India,
Muskaan Complex, Plot No. 3, B-2, Vasant Kunj, New Delhi 110 070
Phone: 91-11-4176-1620 • *Fax:* 91-11-4176-1630 • www.hayhouse.co.in

Distributed in Canada by:
Raincoast Books, 2440 Viking Way, Richmond, B.C. V6V 1N2
Phone: 1-800-663-5714 • *Fax:* 1-800-565-3770 • www.raincoast.com

Access New Knowledge.
Anytime. Anywhere.

Learn and evolve at your own pace with the world's leading experts.

www.hayhouseU.com